DEFENCE WORKS SERVICES
MINISTRY OF DEFENCE

Defence Works Design Guides

Children's play areas design guide

London : HMSO

Children's Play Area Design Guide

First edition Crown Copyright 1992
Second Edition 1995
ISBN 0 11 772459 9

WRITTEN BY THE NATIONAL PLAYING FIELDS ASSOCIATION FOR DEFENCE WORKS SERVICES

Contents

Foreword

This publication's second edition is intended to assist Property Managers, their Works Service Managers (WSMs) and their Establishment Works Consultants (EWCs) in addressing their responsibilities for children's play provision. The publication has been revised in accordance with current practice and feedback received from existing guide users. It focuses on MOD sites within the UK and overseas and acts as the main publication to be used in relation to children's play provision within MOD areas.

It is based on the latest advice from the National Playing Fields Association on the minimum national standards for Children's Outdoor Playing Space within civilian communities and is especially adapted to meet the specific requirements of MOD areas.

This second edition differs from the first in a number of significant ways:-

- It replaces the criteria of a minimum area per 1000 population in favour of a walking time distance between home and three new categories of formal children's outdoor playing space, now recognised as established practice within the UK.

- The previous three categories of formal play areas ie: toddler (children up to 4 years); junior (children between 4 & 8 years); major (primarily children 8 to 14 years) have been superseded by three new categories with the acronyms LAPs, LEAPs & NEAPs. Whilst still based on the appropriate needs of toddler, junior and major age ranges greater importance is placed on the degree of supervision and accessibility criteria required.

- Photographs and illustrations have been introduced to provide visual as well as written assistance.

- The section on inspection and maintenance has been expanded.

- All costs quoted are taken from the 1995 NPFA Cost Guide, and are valid at date of publication.

All queries relating to the application of the guide should be directed to:

Technical Services Directorate
Defence Works Services
Ministry of Defence
PO Box 1734
Rectory Road
Sutton Coldfield
West Midlands B75 7QB

Acknowledgements

This, the second edition of the Children's Play Area Design Guide, has been produced by Defence Works Services in conjunction with Jean M Wenger of the National Playing Fields Association, Richard Greenwood and Andy Wilson-Chalon of NPFA Playground Services Ltd and Ian Watts of Defence Works Services.

The first edition was produced by P.J.Heseltine and Jean M Wenger of the National Playing Fields Association in conjunction with Col. R A Crawley and with the assistance of the late Anne Armstrong of Soldier magazine, Alan Browne, Consultant SMP group, Clive Cain of Defence Works Services, Sharon Hughes of Earthkids and Bill Sanderson of London Borough of Newham.

The authors wish additionally to thank the children and the Families Housing and Welfare Service of Aldershot Garrison, for their help with the publication of photographs contained in the guide.

Introduction

SCOPE

This guide provides the main publication and source of advice to be used by:-

- Property Managers and Project Managers for general guidance
- EWCs for guidance on inspections
- WSMs for design, procurement, installation, maintenance, repair and safety checks

for children's play areas within the UK and overseas.

NON TECHNICAL SUMMARY

Children under fifteen represent 20% of the population of the United Kingdom. They are the greatest users of the outdoor environment and are, consequently, those in greatest need of good quality play opportunities from the environment. The quality of what they learn and receive from the environment, and arguably therefore, the quality of what they become, is dependent to a great extent on the quality of what is provided for them.

Children living on some Ministry of Defence (MOD) Married Quarters Estates can also face problems not normally encountered in purely civilian communities such as:

- Isolation
- The transient nature of occupancy
- One-parent families for periods of up to twelve months
- Security considerations

They are therefore especially in need of access to high quality environments for play and recreation.

Unfortunately the majority of play areas on MOD estates still contain old and outdated equipment, no longer reflecting either the needs of modern children or the recent upsurge in play area design and technology. As a result they are often underused and vandalised - to the detriment of all residents of married quarters (MQ) estates - but particularly to the children they are meant to serve.

It is therefore important for these essential amenities to be upgraded or replaced as soon as possible with the available funds within Property Managers' budgets. If necessary this may need to be done by instituting a rolling programme. In so doing, each play area should be viewed as a key element of the MQ estate as a whole and as part of a wider programme of children's education and recreation within the Services' environment.

It is appreciated that many, perhaps the majority of commanders and staffs have little experience of the subject and this guide has consequently been designed to provide an overview of current thinking on play area design and equipment (in Chapters 1-3). Details of how Property Managers and their Works Service Managers (primarily) can select and order the most appropriate play facilities for each type of MQ estate are in Chapters 4 & 5. Guidance and information on inspection for the Establishment Works Consultant (EWC) has been detailed within Chapter 5 Stage 8.

It should however, be remembered that opportunities for children's play arise throughout MQ estates and not just in a formal equipped play area, however modern. The infrastructure of the complete estate should therefore be considered in this context and the imagination of all concerned used to make the best possible use of existing natural and man-made features.

Of tremendous concern is the possibility of a potential accident to a child in a playground. Thankfully increased amounts of data are now being compiled to advise on the seriousness of accidents together with where and how they are occurring.

Above all it should be remembered that a playground needs to be provided with stimulating and exciting items if children are to use it. If the playground becomes empty of equipment or boring, children will seek their play opportunities elsewhere. Such places include potentially dangerous and undesirable locations such as pavements, roads, garage blocks, motor pools etc.

To ensure the playground remains in a safe and satisfactory condtion it is essential to establish and implement a regular programme of inspections and maintenance. Refer to Chapter 5 Section 8 for further details.

1 The Play Environment

1.1 FORMAL PLAY AREAS

Formal children's outdoor playing spaces (COPS) are essentially designed to cater for specific age groupings within the range of 4 to 14 years. However, children do not fit into prearranged categories; thus, anticipated use by younger and older children has been catered for within each category.

Fig. 1.1 Formal play

The three new categories of COPS are detailed in Chapter 3, where besides providing recommendations on the minimum standards for size, content and general safety features emphasis is placed on supervision and accessibility criteria.

Whilst the majority of Service children fall into the 'from birth to approximately 14 years age range, many families have older teenage children. In America and Germany there have been various experiments with providing specific playgrounds for such teenagers. However, there are leadership and insurance difficulties with this type of provision. Nevertheless some appropriate provision that does not require close supervision in the form of wheeled play, kickabouts and outdoor meeting places for teenagers is included in the notes contained in Annex E. If more ambitious or specialised provision is considered necessary such as BMX cycle tracks or Skateboard parks then specialist advice should be sought, see Annex A.

1.2 INFORMAL PLAY AREAS

In addition to the formal, specifically designed playground there is a need to identify the casual or informal places where children play, such as waste land, and to protect and manage this space for informal use as far as possible. The importance and value of this type of space in child development cannot be overstressed as there is an increasing amount of research evidence to indicate the crucial nature of 'private' space for children. However, it is appreciated that such areas may be difficult to provide and manage on MOD property and a pragmatic approach will often be required.

1.2.1 Ground modelling

Associated with such informal play areas is the concept of ground modelling (Figure 1.2) which can affect both the user and those residents living adjacent to each site. Mounding provides opportunities to improve play and a barrier to noise. Clearly, mounds and hollows present play opportunities in their own right and should be retained wherever possible as ground modelling is a costly and time consuming operation. Their creation or adaptation can allow such equipment as an embankment slide to be installed. Hollows should be visible to casual observation by adults for obvious safety reasons.

Ground Modelling should also be considered for equipped play areas.

Mounding should, ideally, be based on the following principles:

Fig. 1.2 Ground modelling in informal play area

- The height and shape should be dictated by the function and the age groups of the children most likely to be using it. As a general rule the following heights should be aimed for:

  Toddlers - up to 2.5 metres

  Other children - up to 5 metres

- Side slopes should not exceed 30° so as to reduce the potential for ground erosion and the serious maintenance and safety problems of cutting steep grass embankments.

- Shape: Circular mounds are most common but alternative shapes and additional mounds can provide better play opportunities if linked with equipment in various ways.

- Timing: Ideally mounds should be constructed adapted and grassed at least 18 months before any play equipment is installed to allow for good grass establishment and possible construction settlement.

1.2.2 Hard landscaping

Many established and potential playground sites contain existing areas of hardstanding (concrete, tarmacadam, bricks, granite setts etc). These are generally unsuitable for adaptation to play needs other than as:

- Access to formal play areas
- Paths
- Ball games or wheeled toy areas
- Areas of heavy use where grass may be eroded - except in association with playground equipment (where impact absorbing surfacing should be used).

Such 'hard landscaping' should therefore be avoided as a general rule although some features may be utilised for purely decorative purposes or as adjuncts to sand or water play areas for removing sand and water from feet and shoes. Existing tarmac and concrete surfaces can, if in good condition, be utilised for the base of synthetic impact absorbing surfaces (see chapter 4 on play area surfaces).

Fig. 1.3 Hard landscaping

1.3 THE WIDER PLAY ENVIRONMENT

1.3.1 Parental involvement

In addition to formal and casual opportunities for play within the physical environmental, the inclusion of adults in children's play is crucial to their healthy development. Such playwork aspects can be achieved through the provision of:

- Mother and toddler clubs
- Pre-school playgrounds
- Kid's Clubs (out of school provision)
- Holiday play schemes
- Play stores
- Junior and youth clubs
- Sport and recreation facilities

The majority of these facilities are beyond the scope of MOD provision and the terms of reference of this guide. However, one element, the Play Store, should be borne in mind by Property Managers when planning the development of play areas within MQ estates.

1.3.2 Play stores

On certain playgrounds the provision of a play store can provide added opportunities for play development. Such stores contain a variety of play materials which may be used by children under the supervision and stimulation of adults, preferably committed parents from adjacent MQs.

Play stores should be strongly constructed and as secure as possible. Commercial lorry style containers may be suitable. A basic range of play materials should be provided, under local arrangements and at minimum cost. These can include:

- Wheeled toys,
- Sand and water trays,
- Gymnastic mats (not for use as an impact absorbing surface),
- Bats and balls
- Art and craft materials

Local Housing Commandants should consider asking residents living near the play store to form a small group to oversee the store and its contents. Keys should be provided for several of them and local opening hours left to their discretion.

1.3.3 Informal features

The whole of the establishment should be viewed as a place in which children play and informal features should be identified and enhanced throughout MQ estates wherever possible. These might be in the form of general environmental features such as:

- Low walls (below 600mm) capable of balancing activities
- Features such as barriers if designed for gymnastic activities or of a design such that they may by used as an agility item, should be provided with an appropriate impact absorbing surface
- Patterns in hard paved areas (not pavements beside roads or other areas where vehicles are parked or moving) to assist wheeled play and games such as hopscotch
- The forming of counters into grass areas and the inclusion of planting to encourage games
- Provision of informal seating points, for example low walls, and safe and secure boulders and old tree stumps
- Appropriate planting schemes

Ideally, such facilities should be included as near to the focal point of MQ estates as possible; on flow paths around the housing area and adjacent to community facilities.

1.3.4 Street play

The importance attached to vehicular traffic has had a major impact on the play, mobility and safety of children. There is considerable evidence to demonstrate that improvement in the quality of children's play and in the general life of the neighbourhood results when appropriate measures to calm traffic are taken.

Fig. 1.4 Street play

No matter how good the formal or informal play area may be, many children will spend some time playing immediately adjacent to their home. Property Managers should therefore consider taking appropriate measures to create areas of vehicle/child compatibility wherever possible in both existing and, more particularly, in new estates.

This system commonly known as a "Woonerf", which is the Dutch for "Living Yard", imposes strict controls on cars in streets and roads within housing areas to allow the provision of extra play areas for children. Further details on incorporation of such designs can be found in the NPFA publication "The Six Acre Standard".

Such measures could include:

- Widened pavements
- Planting
- Banked and raised corners
- Inclusion of bollards, lampposts and planting areas alongside estate roads
- Changes in surface texture
- Alternative parking, Cul-de-sacs, Speed tables etc all tied in as appropriate to the estate security plans
- Improved lighting

Further guidance on the design of roads and footpaths and traffic calming measures within estates can be found in the DWS Parking and Access manual.

1.3.5 Planting

A further important element in the play environment as a whole is the adaptation of existing trees and shrubs, or more usually, the planting of new species to enhance existing, or planned, formal and informal play areas. Such soft landscaping, although comparatively expensive, provides an enhanced quality of life for every member of a MQ estate out of all proportion to the cost involved and should therefore be kept in mind by Property Managers, particularly when planning new play area projects. Ideally planting schemes should be designed to provide:

- A variety of play opportunities
- Micro-climate modification, for example shelter, windbreaks etc
- Seasonal changes (changes of colour, flowering and fruiting)
- Assistance with drainage
- Erosion control
- Sensory variation, for example planting which provides different scents and textures
- Aesthetic value
- Enclosures
- Craft or culinary opportunities
- Wild life habitats

For further guidance on planting, refer to DWS Landscaping manual.

1.3.6 Focus points

Finally, in order to assist children with their development of social and spatial mapping ability, it is recommended that recognisable landmarks are positioned throughout communities in the form of sculptures, murals etc. There is a German development, "Spielpunkt", which entails developing large individual play items/sculptures at key points in the environment to aid this process. While it is appreciated that such enhancements may not suit either the tastes or budgets of some Property Managers, their potential for child development and, arguably, the aesthetic value to the MQ estate as a whole, should be borne in mind.

2 Play area siting and design

2.1 INTRODUCTION

This chapter deals with the minimum standards required for location, content, size, general safety and site requirements for the three categories of formal children's outdoor playing space (COPS). The play equipment itself and the type of surface on which it stands are dealt with in subsequent chapters for ease of reference. It is emphasised that the recommendations are minimum standards based on the latest national advice from the National Playing Fields Association and especially adapted to meet the specific requirements of MOD areas.

It should also be remembered that most Service estates contain a small number of children with mobility difficulties and that such children deserve the same facilities as their peers. However, as a general principle, if children with mobility difficulties can reach the equipment provided, they are usually able to use standard items. It is therefore the pathways and surfaces that need to reflect the limited mobility of such children and this should be taken into account.

2.2 ACCESSIBILITY

Accessibility is a very important consideration in the provision of children's outdoor playing space. Children invariably play outdoors and close to home. If no purpose built facilities exist sufficiently close to home then children will use inappropriate places that may be unsafe or cause a disturbance to others.

The best measure of accessibility is the time it takes a child to leisurely walk from home to the facility without the temptation or necessity to cross dangerous physical barriers.

Within the descriptions of the three categories of children's outdoor playing space are the recommended walking times along with an equivalent 'pedestrian' and 'straight-line' distance. Measurement of the shortest, safe pedestrian link is a far more reliable guide than the straight-line distance in determining walking time.

In civilian residential areas the physical barriers to accessibility such as main roads, canals, railway line and isolated areas normally remain constant throughout the year. In MOD areas where 'zones & routes' are restricted from time to time careful consideration needs to be given to determining the shortest safe access.

As a guideline, the shortest safe pedestrian route chosen to determine the walking time to a play facility should be when it can reasonably be anticipated it will not be restricted for more than 3 hours per day between 9.00am and dusk, nor for more than one full day per week. Restricted times should be advertised well in advance to children, parents and guardians of children whenever possible, by posters and circular letter. There will be occasions when the chosen access has to be restricted for longer periods; in which case, special arrangements to escort children to play facilities may be appropriate.

2.3 SUPERVISION

Whilst the three categories of children's outdoor playing space relate to 'unsupervised and unaccompanied' use by particular age groups, it is recognised that it is both desirable and inevitable that slightly older and younger children than those the facility is primarily intended for, will use them.

2.4 THE THREE CATEGORIES OF FORMAL CHILDREN'S OUTDOOR PLAYING SPACE (COPS)

Included in this guide are recommendations for the provision of different types of play areas. These provide for a range of age groups and appropriate facilities for their needs. Most frequent, and therefore closest to home, are small areas for younger children. Less frequent, and more likely to be further away are larger areas for older children. All houses should be within the safe prescribed walking time of each type of children's outdoor playing space. The existing playground provision, as well as new or required provision, should be analysed against these categories to establish the current and required needs of the estate.

The three categories of play are:

- Local Areas for Play (toddlers 0-6 years) - LAPs
- Local Equipped Areas for Play (juniors 6-8 years plus toddlers) - LEAPs
- Neighbourhood Equipped Areas for Play (major 8-14 years plus juniors and toddlers) - NEAPs

The terms 'Active' & 'Buffer' Zones are used in the following descriptions of LAPs, LEAPs & NEAPs.

Their definitions are:-

ACTIVE ZONE - is the area of land specifically designated for children to use for play purposes. It may or may not include play equipment.

BUFFER ZONE - is that area surrounding the Active Zone.
It is designed to discourage children from using it for actual play purposes, and is provided solely to protect adjacent land users from potential disturbance through the existence of the play facility.

All three types of play area are ideally located at a single location and separated only by the design layout. The sole reason for requiring separate locations is to ensure the accessibility criteria are met.

Where a NEAP (major 8-14 years plus) and LEAP (juniors 6-8 years and toddlers 0-6 years) are combined at a single location then a saving on the total number of types of play equipment can be achieved. i.e. Eleven types of play equipment at a combined NEAP and LEAP achieves the same objective as eight at a NEAP and five at a LEAP - a capital saving on two play items.

See Annex E for further information. Notes for a kickabout areas, wheeled play opportunities and meeting places are contained at the end of the section.

2.4.1 LAP (local area for play) - toddlers 0- 6 years

A LAP is a small unsupervised area of open space specifically designated for toddlers and young children for play activities not requiring play equipment

Location: Within 1 minute's walking time. i.e. 100m walking distance or 60m straight line distance.

Target Users: Mainly for 0 to 6 year olds, The needs of children with disabilities such as mobility and sensory problems.

Fig. 2.1 Example of a LAP

NOTE: Children over the age of 6 are likely to cause some disturbance to adjacent residents; therefore, the LAP design should discourage such use by limiting the size and opportunity for activities attractive to older children.

Characteristics: Small low key games area preferably with 'demonstrative' play features. Size: Active Zone -100 m2, Total (inc Buffer Zone) - 400 m2 (0.04 ha).

Nearest House: 5m from edge of activity zone to ground floor windows of residential properties in full view of the activity zone. Gable end or other exposed house walls should be protected from use for ball games, e.g. a 1m strip of dense planting.

2.4.2 LEAP (local equipped area for play) - juniors 6 - 8 yrs, plus toddlers 0 - 6 yrs

A LEAP is an unsupervised play area primarily equipped for children of early school age ie juniors, and also providing an equipment range for toddlers. (Figure 2.2)

Fig. 2.2 Example of a LEAP

Location: Within 5 minute's walking distance of home. i.e. 400m walking distance or 240m straight line distance.

Target Users: Mainly for children from 6 to 8, with consideration given to children from birth to 6, children slightly older than 8 and children with special needs.

Characteristics: At least 5 items of play equipment and a small flat games area.

Size: Active Zone - 400 m2, Total (inc Buffer Zone) - 3,600 m2 (0.36 ha)
Nearest House: 20m from edge of Activity Zone to property boundary.

2.4.3 NEAP (neighbourhood equipped area for play) - major 8 - 14 yrs, plus juniors 6 - 8 yrs, and toddlers 0 - 6 yrs

A NEAP is an unsupervised play area primarily equipped for older children (majors) and young teenagers. Equipment for juniors and toddlers should also be provided.

Location: Within 15 minutes walking time of home. i.e. approximately 1000m walking distance or 600m straight line distance.

Fig. 2.3 Example of a NEAP

Target Users: Mainly for children between 8 and 14, with consideration for slightly younger and older children and those with special needs.

Characteristics: About 8 items of play equipment, plus kickabout and wheeled play opportunities, and seating for accompanying adults and for teenagers to use as a meeting place.

Size: Active Zone - 1,000 m2 , Total (inc Buffer Zone) - 8,500 m2 (0.85 ha).
Nearest House: 30 m from edge of Activity Zone to property boundary.

2.4.4 SAFETY

Adequate safety measures should be taken to minimise the risk of road related accidents and potential dangers from nearby water courses, electricity cables and railway lines. The play facility should contain informal surveillance in the form of adjacent housing physically overlooking the site and/or being adjacent to routes frequently used by passers by.

2.5 ANCILLARY ITEMS FOR PLAY AREAS

2.5.1 Fencing

The overall play area should be fenced primarily to exclude dogs, although security requirements, particularly for major areas, should also be borne in mind. Fencing should extend beyond the equipment and include the casual play area.

An open fence 1-1.2m high of vertical barriers or with weld-mesh infill is recommended. Kickabout areas will require a 2.75-3m high weld-mesh style or heavy gauge chain link fence.

Fig. 2.4 Fencing

Fencing should never contain barbed or razor wire. Where for security this is required, special care should be taken and a second inner fence provided to prevent access to the barbed wire.

2.5.2 Gates

Wherever play areas are fenced a minimum of two access points are recommended with details as follows:

- Two self-closing gates (1.2m wide) will help ensure site security and child safety. Gates should be sufficiently robust to withstand children swinging on them. Additional lockable gates suitable for vehicle maintenance entry should also be provided.

- Care should be taken to ensure that the gates do not “slam” and thereby cause a hazard to children’s fingers. Additionally care should be taken to ensure that sufficient clearance between the gate’s stile and the gate post is present at all times. A number of serious accidents have occurred on playgrounds where children’s fingers have been injured or severed.

Figure 2.5 Illustration of potential crush point.

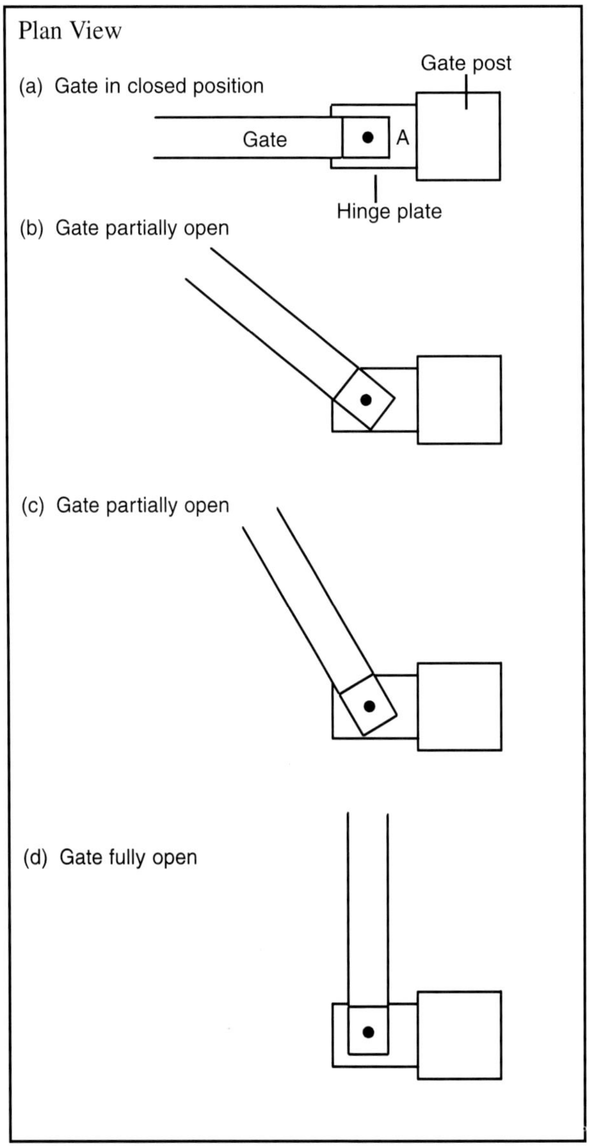

Figure 2.6 Illustration of BS 5696 Finger Probe used to test compliance as required in Part 2, 4.7 (a) and (b).

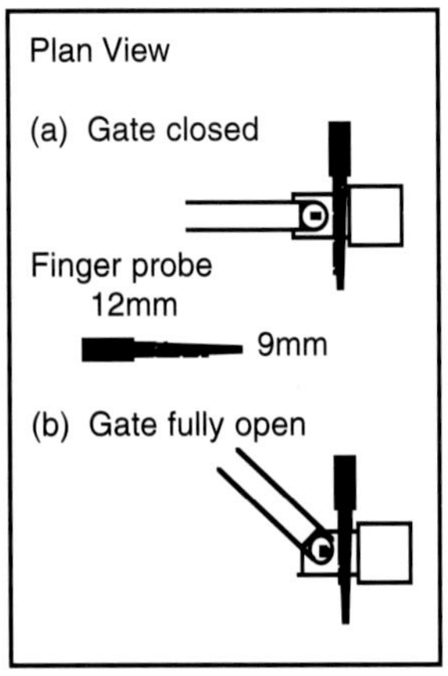

(The probe tapers from 12mm to 9mm over its length)

As the gate opens, the gap between the hinge plate and the gate post reduces creating a "pinch point". The problem is exacerbated by the square edge of the hinge plate. If a rounded plate is used (Figure 2.6), the gap at point "A" remains constant.

Figure 2.7 shows a gate hinge that has has been associated with a crush injury. A possible solution incorporating a rounded hinge plate is shown in Figure 2.8.

- Gates should open outwards.

On some sites it may be possible to provide more exciting entrances, such as clatter bridges, or ramps. However, it should be appreciated that children tend to take the most direct route and entrances should be sited with this in mind. These may also restrict access for children with disabilities.

On new playgrounds, particularly those on large sites with many access routes, careful consideration of access points should be given to avoid unofficial entrances being made.

Indeed, after the site has been in use for six months, it may be necessary to reassess both access and traffic flows and, if necessary, to re-site them.

Fig. 2.7 Potential entrapment

Fig. 2.8 No entrapment present

2.5.3 Signs

It is recommended that suitable robust signs (see Figure 2.4) should be provided at the entrance to each play area indicating;

- Contact for reporting accidents/faults
- Dog exclusion
- A suitable logo

Fig. 2.9/2.10 Seating

2.5.4 Seating

Seating is essential to stimulate social play among children and to encourage parents to meet and stay on the playground. Parental accompaniment usually provides informal supervision of the site. Whenever possible seating should be provided on all sites appropriate to the age-groups for which they are designed. Ideally, seating should be located in sheltered areas with some shade available for hot weather and should consist of the following:

- Toddler play: equipment and sand play areas.- Small-scale seating and tables
- Junior and major: Grouped seating for social play, (such as picnic benches)
- Adults: Robust, all weather seating should be located adjacent to play equipment and sand play areas. It should be remembered that children are often only allowed to use the playground for as long as their parent remains. A comfortable seat helps everybody.

2.5.5 Footpaths and cycleways

No matter how good the design of a play area, unless children can reach it easily, quickly and safely it is unlikely to be fully used. It is therefore important that associated footpaths and cycleways are planned to provide a direct and logical route to each facility, taking account of established traffic flows where these exist and avoiding scenic or circular detours.

2.5.6 Special needs

It is important to remember that a small minority of children on Service estates may suffer from disabilities and that this should not necessarily prevent them from using the play facilities which have been provided. As a general principle, if such children can reach the equipment they are usually able to use standard items, it is clearly important to design both footpaths and surfaces for children with mobility difficulties in mind.

Fig. 2.11 Requirements for children with special needs

On at least one access for children with a disability, the main pathways should be at least 1.2m wide and have a maximum slope over distances of up to 10m of 1 in 12, after which a horizontal section of 1.8m minimum should be provided. For longer distances a slope of no more than 1 in 20 is advised. Overhead clearances should be 2m.

2.5.7 Cycles

Cycles should be discouraged on equipped playgrounds. Many children arrive at playgrounds by cycle therefore cycle racks or stands should be provided. These should be of a design that allows the cycles to be secured by the rider's chain and lock.

2.5.8 Litter bins and lighting

Fig. 2.12 Litter Bins

The following facilities should be included in the majority of play areas:

- Litter bins should be provided adjacent to seating areas. A regular emptying programme will be required if these are to be fully effective. The requirements of the Environmental Protection Act 1991 should also be noted.

- Lighting on areas away from housing should be considered, especially in conjunction with ball play in the evenings. However, it is appreciated that this is an expensive option which is unlikely to be justified in isolation. A lighting level of 150 lux with a minimum diversity of 70% is advised. Illumination may need to be provided from several directions to avoid shadows cast by structures.

2.5.9 Dogs

While dog fouling is both unpleasant and a health hazard, it is difficult to control on an open MQ estate. It is therefore important to provide a fence to the overall site area and display the appropriate enforcement signs as already indicated.

Commanders may also wish to consider the passing of local orders excluding dogs from certain recreation grounds and informal play areas although it is recommended that EWC advice is obtained first to ensure that such orders do not run, where appropriate, contrary to local authority policy or existing byelaws. It should be noted that dog bites are a common form of playground injury.

The requirements of the Environmental Protection Act 1991 should also be noted as this may be applicable within certain areas of the establishment. This Act provides for Local Authorities to designate areas of land, including public open space, sports areas, recreation grounds, playing fields, parks and children's playgrounds as to be kept to a certain level of cleanliness in respect of litter. Dog faeces is classified under the Act as litter. If a designated area is not kept to the required level of cleanliness a substantial fine can be imposed on the site owner or operator.

It is important to provide overall advice where dogs are excluded or welcomed. To install a dog restriction on certain sites without providing information on where dogs can be exercised provides confusion and can lead to unnecessary conflict with dog owners. The National Playing Fields Association provide detailed advice in their publication "Dogs and Recreation Policy Guidelines". In summary their recommendations are firmly for clean, pleasant and safe environments for children's play and sporting activities. It calls on all responsible organisations, particularly owners and managers of recreational land, to work urgently towards achieving higher environmental and safety standards in this important area.
On recreational sites, the NPFA's guidelines are:

NO DOGS (except guide dogs)

- in equipped playgrounds
- on sport pitches and outdoor sports facilities such as courts and greens
- on school playing fields or grounds, and recreational land primarily used by schools
- on areas intended for, or commonly used by, children at play, such as grassed and hard surfaced areas within housing estates

DOGS OK

- in defined parts of larger parks and on commons, unless there is good reason to exclude them, or to insist on leashing
- in dedicated dog exercise areas.

Fig. 2.13 Dog ban sign

3 Play equipment selection

3.1 INTRODUCTION

This chapter describes a basic range of equipment suitable for each of the three types of play areas, the Standard to which it should be supplied and various information relevant to potential suppliers.

3.2 PLAY EQUIPMENT RANGES

3.2.1 LAPs (toddlers 0-6 yrs)

A LAP does not have any traditional play equipment provided; it is an area of land designated and made available for play. However it should have a number of features to encourage toddlers and other young children to use it. Such features may promote activities like games of tag, hopscotch, French cricket or play with small toys. They should be provided with eye catching visual devices such as a sculpture or mushroom seats. All LAPs should have seating for carers and be surrounded by a low guard rail. LAPs offer significant design opportunities for improving the aesthetic and planting opportunities of the estate.

Fig. 3.1 Local area for play (LAP)

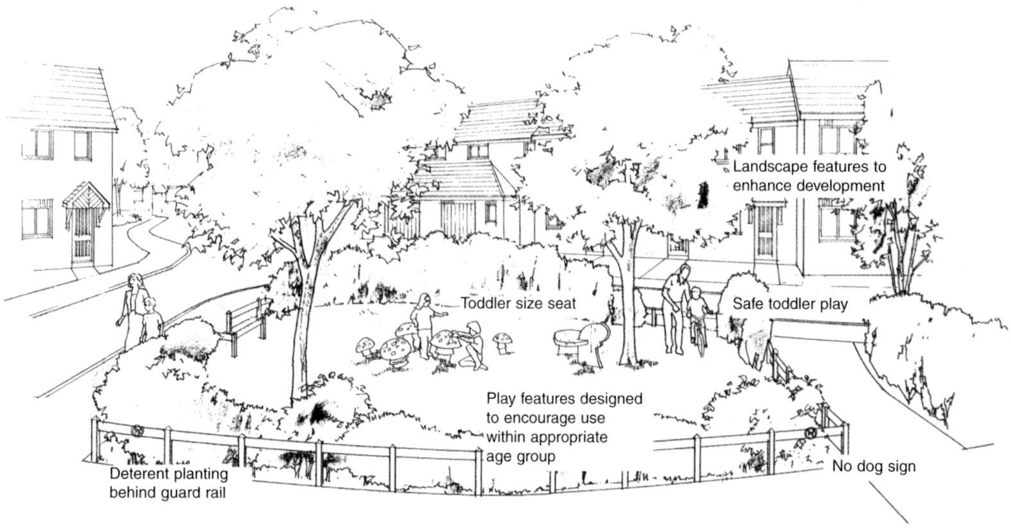

3.2.2 LEAPs (junior 6-8 yrs, plus toddlers 0 - 6 yrs)

These play areas will serve a wide range of abilities and care must be taken to ensure that a fair mix of opportunities are provided. The mixing of toddlers directly with Juniors is not recommended as the age and ability of these children can be considerably different. A LEAP should be subdivided to provide two distinct sections, one for juniors and the other for toddlers. Unless there is a remarkably higher number of Toddlers within the catchment area the Junior range or equipment should always be the larger numerically. At least 5 items of equipment offering a range of activities for toddlers and juniors.

The Junior section of the LEAP should contain eight to ten and as many as possible of the following activities, of which two should be moving items.

- Balancing*. jumping, climbing,* sliding, rocking, rotating, bridges,* ground graphics,* scrambling,* swinging, gliding, agility,* sitting, etc.

No more than five of the asterisked activities should be considered for combining in one multi-play piece of equipment.

Multi-play items should be studied carefully as many may provide fewer play opportunities than can be achieved for the same amount of money spent on individual items and designed carefully into the site.

Items of equipment should be provided in at least two primary colours. In addition, each LEAP should also contain a general play space surfaced with grass.

The toddler section of the LEAP will have at least three to five of the following activities of which one to two should be moving items of equipment.

- Balancing, jumping, play house, sandbox, sand structure, water play, climbing, rocking, sliding, ground graphics, crawling, rotating, swinging, sitting etc.

The equipment selected should be provided in at least 2 primary colours.

Fig. 3.2 Local equipped area for play (LEAP)

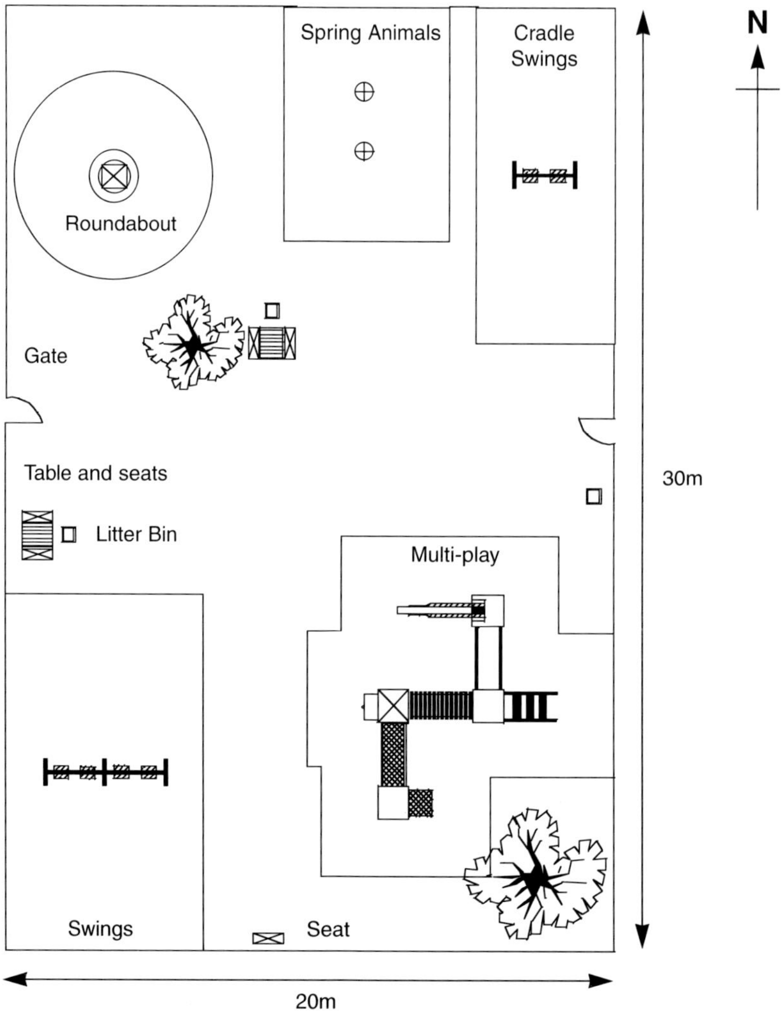

Fig. 3.2 shows toddler and junior areas combined as a LEAP, with equipment shown within their minimum use zones. The estimated cost of the above, depending on supplier, materials and extras, would be approximately £36,000 to include installation.

Please note: This an indicative layout, and should not be used as a standard design.

3.2.3 NEAPs (major 8 - 14 yrs, plus junior 6 - 8 yrs and toddler 0 - 6 yrs)

Facilities in a NEAP should, ideally, cater for all children up to 14 years or age and should therefore have zones set aside for major, junior and toddler children. NEAPs should contain at least 8 items of play equipment with as many as possible (15 are recommended) of the activities provided for the LEAP with a substantial proportion of the range aimed at the major child range. It is important that juniors and toddlers have sections provided with equipment that is most suited to their age and ability, so as to provide a facility that can serve the whole range of the estate's children. A large grassed area should also be provided for casual games and general running about. For older children the following activities are particularly recommended: aerial runways, single point suspension swings, wheeled play areas for skateboards, roller skates and BMX bikes and a ball play area normally 500-600 sq m.

Figure 3.3 Neighbourhood equipped area for play (NEAP)

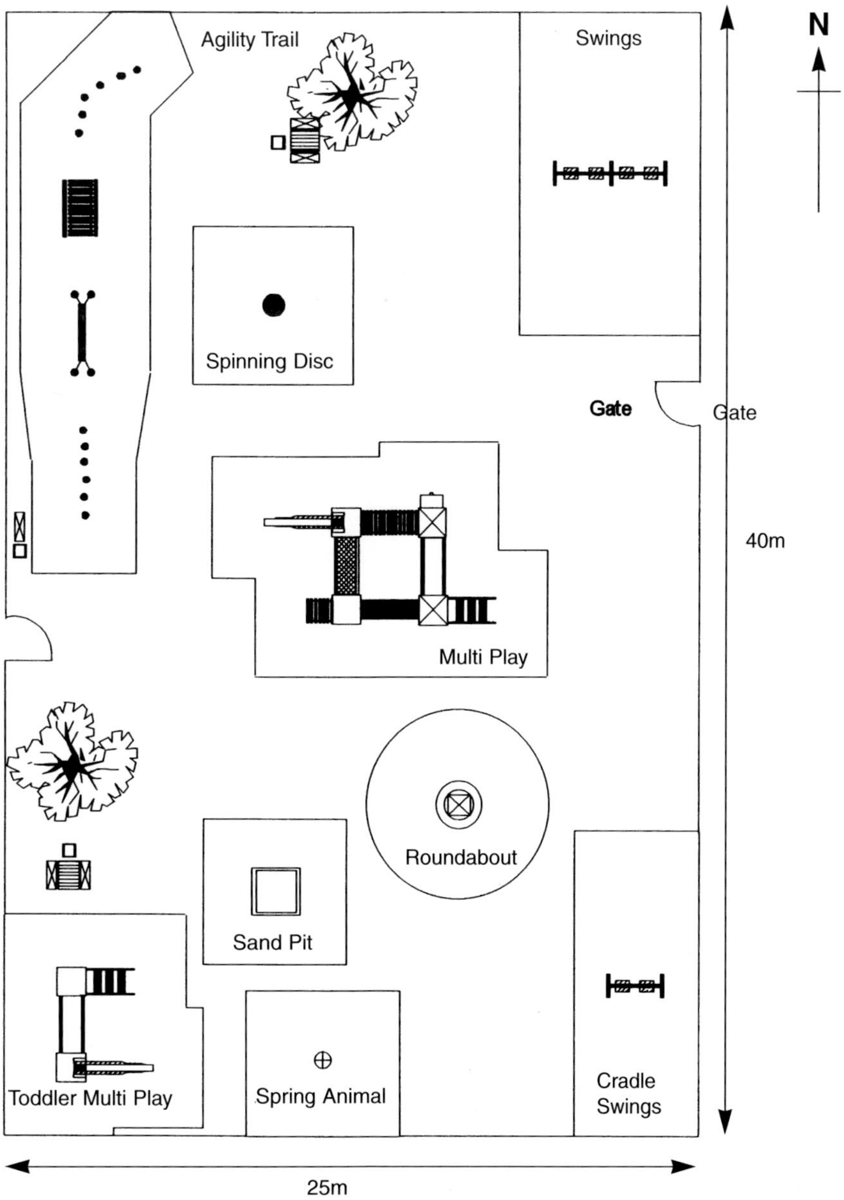

The estimated cost of the above would be in the region of £60,000.

The above is an indicative layout, and should not be used as a standard design. Most manufacturers will provide their own plans when tendering for new developments.

3.2.4 Impact absorbing surfaces

All equipment with a fall height in excess of 600mm should be sited on an impact absorbing surface so as to reduce the severity of any injury resulting from a fall. Such surfaces should always be installed at the same time as a new item of equipment.

Existing items without a suitable impact absorbing surface should be carefully assessed - see section 4.6

3.3 PLAYGROUND EQUIPMENT - BUDGET COST INFORMATION

Fig. 3.4 Agility

Fig. 3.5 Multiplay

Fig. 3.6 Rocking

The following budget costs are taken from the NPFA Cost Guide 1995 edition and include information on sports, buildings and children's play facilities. Also incorporated are listings of main contractors and suppliers as supplied to and used by the Building Cost Information Service of the RICS and the Sports Council. It is prepared and revised annually by the NPFA Technical Department.

The following include supply, delivery, installation, and impact absorbing surfacing where necessary. Items for Toddlers are towards the lower end of the price range. All estimated costs are exclusive of VAT.

AGILITY - ladders, climbing frames, large climbers	£2,000 - £35,000
BALANCING - log steps, balance beams, chain walks	£250 - £2,600
GROUND GRAPHICS - painted surfaces, hopscotch etc	£250 - £800
SWINGING - tunnels, bridges	£600 - £1,800
GLIDING - aerial runway	£4,000 - £10,000
MULTIPLAY - combination item incorporating many activities	£7,000 - £50,000

Fig. 3.7 Sliding

Fig 3.8 Climbing

Fig. 3.9 Ground graphics

PLAYHUT
£700 - £4,500

ROCKING - springs, rocking horse	£500 - £3,000
ROTATING - pirouettes, dizzy disc, roundabouts	£2,000 - £4,500
SANDBOX	£500 - £1,500
SANDSTRUCTURE - cranes, pulley	£900 - £1,500
SITTING - play tables, play house, children's seats	£200 - £3,000
SLIDING	£3,000 - £9,000
SWINGING - single, group	£2,000 - £8,000
WATER PLAY - sprays, water tables paddling pools	£300 - £20,000

Fig. 3.10 Social play facilities

3.4 EQUIPMENT LOCATED IN HOT OR COLD CLIMATES

Given the opportunity children will play anywhere. However extremes of cold or heat will require a more careful selection of equipment and the layout/design of the playground.

- COLD CLIMATES: Whilst the saying "there's no such thing as being cold, only being incorrectly dressed" may be true, in some situations direct skin to metal contact can cause skin adhesion accidents. In very cold climatic conditions, ranges of playground equipment and their surface finishes should be selected with this knowledge. Alternative surfaces eg timber elements or some plastic coverings can reduce this problem. In snow, moving items, eg swings and roundabouts should be immobilised or removed as ground clearances can be severely reduced causing possible trip and entrapment hazards. Often in these climates slides should face south to capture the maximum sunshine to help warm the metal surfaces.

- HOT CLIMATES: The playground layout and design of the equipment should incorporate the maximum opportunities for shade and minimise as far as possible skin to metal contact points. Whereas in cold climates gloves will protect a child, in hot climates children are unlikely to increase their clothing layers. Again timber elements and some plastic coverings can assist. Large metal surfaces (on slides for example) should face north so as to avoid the direct rays of the sun for as long as possible. Where such surfaces have faced the sun burns have resulted. Hot climates create marvellous opportunities for tactile play with very shallow water and sand.

3.5 POSITIONING OF EQUIPMENT

The NPFA's aim is to encourage a creative and community-involved approach to play area design and they therefore recommend only a few basic principles in the siting of equipment:

3.5.1 Minimum use zone (MUZ)

The Minimum Use Zone (MUZ) indicated by the supplier or by paragraph 3.4 of BS 5696 Part 3 should be adhered to. This refers to the safe positioning area of the equipment. If no figure is given by the supplier the following distance should be applied:

- Static items, at least 1.8m all around
- Moving items, at least 2.4m all around.
- Swings at sides 1.2m fore and aft (0.866 x pivot point to seat surface) + 3.55m

NB The MUZ does not cover exactly the same area as impact absorbing surfaces which is normally 1.75m.

3.5.2 Flow routes

The MUZ of the item when moving in a direct line between activities or moving equipment should not be sited in such a way that children cross entering and leaving the playground.

3.5.3 Equipment linking

The possibilities for linking equipment to enhance certain types of games (ie chase and tag games) should be considered. This may be achieved by other items of equipment, landscape features, ground graphics, etc.

3.5.4 Individual items

Sand Play Areas: Sand play should be placed in quiet windfree areas capable of being shaded at midday and early afternoon, with seating for adults nearby. A raised sand box is preferable to a recessed sand pit. In some areas it may be necessary to cover the sand when not in use with a non mesh cover. A sand structure should be provided if funds permit

Fig. 3.11 Water play

- Water Play: In addition to water play structures, such as paddling and splash pools, consideration should be given to the provision of a water playground and/or underground piping for spray attachments.

- Murals: Colour can be brought into a playground through murals - either on walls or ground surfaces. It is important that children should do the painting wherever possible.

- Shapes: Angular shapes can be helpful in stimulating activity, while softer flowing curves can be restful. However, it should be borne in mind that sharp corners, narrow strips and small sections of grass are difficult to clean and mow.

- Materials: Materials should be selected with regard to the site and type of structure whilst a range of textures is recommended, the following guidelines should be applied.

  Static items: Components entering the ground should be of timer construction although subsequent vertical members and other parts may be of timber.

  Moving Items: Metal is recommended for all supports although timber may be used for cladding.

- Colour: The use of colour on playgrounds is important for child development and should be introduced through the equipment, the surfacing, planting and murals as follows:

  Activity Areas: Bright primary colours - reds, yellows, oranges predominating

  Quiet/Rest Areas: Blues and greens predominating.

3.6 EQUIPMENT STANDARDS

It is important that all play area equipment and surfacing meet appropriate standards of safety. All equipment and surfacing should meet British Standard BS 5696, or when not so covered, the German standard DIN 7926 plus the technical recommendations of the National Playing Fields Association.

A European Standard is being prepared by the Central European Standards organisation (CEN) under their playground Technical Committee (TC 136/SC1) although it is anticipated that the first part will not be published before 1996. It will, in due course, automatically replace the national standards of the European and EFTA countries.

Property Managers should not delay action pending this Standard's publication as it will broadly follow the current British and German Standards.

It is recommended that the following phrase should be included in all Tender Specifications:

- "Confirmation should be given in writing that each item of equipment and surfacing when supplied and installed, will meet BS 5696 or where not covered by BS 5696, meet DIN 7926 plus National Playing Fields Association published recommendations in NPFA Technical Advisory Notices"

It is possible to purchase equipment that has been awarded a British Standard Kitemark, there are however a limited number of such items available on the market. Provided that non-kitemarked items are manufactured and installed to conform to BS 5696, this is considered to be satisfactory.

Some items of equipment, whether covered by Standards or not, have given rise to problems and caused sufficient concern to recommend against their continued use or provision. Details of these are published by the NPFA in their Technical Advisory Notices (TANs). Specific guidance on such equipment is given in TAN 27 "Children's playground equipment not recommended by the NPFA". It will be noted that some items may be commonly found on playgrounds and that many of them relate to moving or agility items.

3.7 SELF-BUILD EQUIPMENT

It should be noted that self-build equipment is not a substitute for well made commercially manufactured products. The use of self-build equipment is not recommended.

If they have to be used, such items should create simple additional structures or enhance the use of commercial equipment and landscape features. Like all equipment, self-build equipment has a finite life which is usually much less than that a commercially manufactured item. As a general principle, five years useful life should be anticipated. Property Managers should assess such items carefully to note:

- Standard compliance
- Durability
- Maintenance requirements
- Ease of obtaining and fitting vandalised or replacement parts

Constructors of such equipment should be aware that they may acquire liabilities under consumer protection legislation. Supervised voluntary groups can however often assist in some areas eg excavation and filling of loose fill surfacing areas. Voluntary groups should be encouraged to participate in equipment selection, fund raising and informal supervision of the play area upon completion.

3.8 SELECTION OF SUPPLIERS

3.8.1 Selection criteria

It is recommended that preference is given to companies holding the Quality Assurance Standard BS 5750/EN 29000/ISO 9000. It makes sense from a maintenance and budget viewpoint to standardise on types and ranges of items, for example swings, when their installation is planned over a number of separate play areas within a Command/District/Station.

Play equipment should comply with 3.6 and be primarily of metal construction, especially the main support structure. All equipment should be installed with the appropriate impact absorbing surface.

3.8.2 Product information and names of suppliers

Suppliers should provide the following written information in respect of each item of equipment ordered, an up-to-date list of suppliers of equipment and play area surfaces can be obtained from the NPFA Cost Guide publication, see Annex B.

- Name, product description and date of manufacture
- Written confirmation of compliance with the appropriate standard ie BS 5696 or DIN 7926 plus National Playing Fields Association published recommendations in NPFA Technical Advisory Notices
- Parts list
- Minimum use zones
- Surfacing requirements for impact absorbing surfacing and other surfaced areas
- Assembly instructions
- Installation and operation instructions

- Inspection and maintenance details
- Life expectancy
- Availability period for replacement parts
- Post installation check list
- Normal manufacturer guarantees and warranties

3.8.3 Toddler areas (LEAP or NEAP)

Manufacturers should indicate the suitability of equipment for younger ages. This should cover height, ergonomic requirements and some indication of developmental function. A wide variety of equipment is not required in these areas and standardisation will assist maintenance.

3.8.4 Warranty periods

Suppliers should provide a minimum guarantee period of five years for each item.

3.8.5 Labelling

Equipment should be labelled in accordance with BS 5696 Part 2. On multi-use items, whilst all items should comply with the selected standard, only one item need be labelled.

4 Play area surfaces

4.1 INTRODUCTION

The final element in playground design concerns the essential choice of surfacing. In general terms any play area consists of four distinct surfacing areas:

- Pathways and wheeled toy areas which can be on concrete or macadam or a similar firmly bound smooth surface
- Specialised surfaces for wheeled play, eg BMX, skateboards, roller-skates - normally a hot rolled asphalt surface
- The areas between equipment areas - normally grass
- Areas underneath and around items of equipment

This Chapter deals with the recommended surfaces around items of equipment.

4.2 TYPE OF SURFACES

4.2.1 Natural surfaces

Any item of equipment which has a fall height of less than 600mm does not strictly require an impact absorbing surface. Grass is not, however, suitable for ground immediately under or around equipment. In areas in between equipment and for general run around surfaces it is quite acceptable although on intensively used areas, for example around entrances, grass reinforcement may be necessary or an alternative surface such as macadam.

Grass is not acceptable as an Impact Absorbing Surface (IAS) as it is affected by climatic conditions, eg a dry summer or freezing winter altering the make up of the soil and reducing its impact absorbency. A grass surface under intensive use quickly erodes, losing its surface covering and root growth (which keeps the soil texture open), it then compacts and loses any impact absorbency. Many soils additionally contain a significant stone content which can again adversely affect any impact absorbency a grass surface may have.

4.2.2 Impact absorbing surfaces (IAS)

Any equipment with a fall height in excess of 600mm should be sited on an impact absorbing surface. Such surfaces are of two types, one of which, in certain circumstances, may be more suitable than the other:

- Loose Fill

Materials in this category include: tree bark, sand, pea shingle, light weight ceramics and wood chip. Tree bark of a particle range of between 12 - 38mm is recommended. It is easy to install, effective and relatively cheap but requires daily maintenance plus topping-up. This may make it more expensive than a synthetic surface over an 8-10 year period. Where tree bark is not available, clean washed sand of a particle range 0.25 - 1.5mm may be used, provided it does not contain artificially crushed material or shells (sea shells).

Loose fill surfaces should not be installed under moving items, unless daily checks are made to ensure that surfacing levels are maintained, and requirements to remove any deleterious materials such as glass, can be undertaken.

Fig. 4.1 Loose fill and synthetic surfacing

- Synthetic

Such surfaces, which are becoming increasingly common, are mainly of the tile, carpet, or wet-pour types. They are generally effective, are more permanent than loose-fill and have less maintenance requirements. However, they are initially more expensive.

4.3 SURFACE AREAS

It is unnecessary to surface a complete playground with expensive impact absorbing materials. In some circumstances however, it can be less labour intensive to provide a synthetic or loose fill surface for the whole site. The IAS area for each type of equipment is contained in British Standard BS 5696 Part 3 and can be summarised as follows:

- Static Equipment
  (such as climbing frames). An area extending 1.75m from each of the outer edges of the equipment

- Moving Equipment
  (such as see-saws). An area extending 1.75m beyond the maximum travel limit of the equipment, thence as for static.

- Swings
  Between the internal supports and for a distance in either direction of motion of 0.866 of the distance between swing pivot point and the seat surface plus 1.75m. (The distance of 0.866 represents a swing angle of 60.) This dimension is then doubled to give the overall length of surfacing ie fore/aft.

When a loose fill impact absorbing surface is selected, a minimum depth of 300mm should be provided and maintained. Tree bark is the normal material used and should contain no sharp edges, dust or very large particles. Particle size should ideally be between 12-38mm. Sand should be of an even grain between 0.25 and 1.5mm in size. The material should be contained in a box or pit 300mm deep lined with suitable edging. It may require a porous membrane and/or drainage layer connected to a soakaway or surface water drain. To cater for children with mobility handicaps ramps with a slip resistant covering should ideally be provided between any multiplay structure and the nearest hard pathway. Care should be taken to "marry in" with the surrounding surfaces thereby preventing trip points.

Fig. 4.2 Loose fill surfacing installation

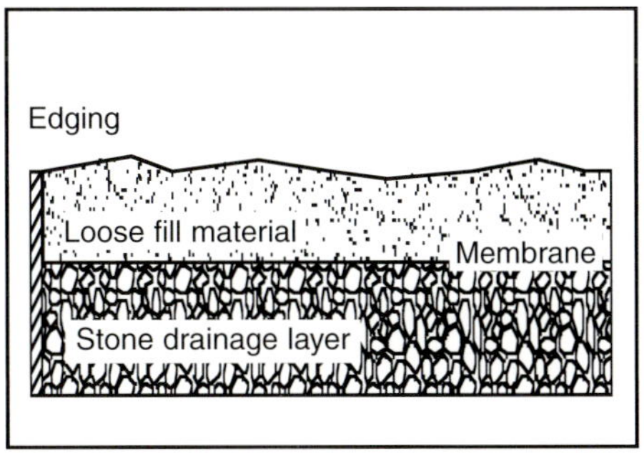

Fig. 4.3 Synthetic surfacing installation

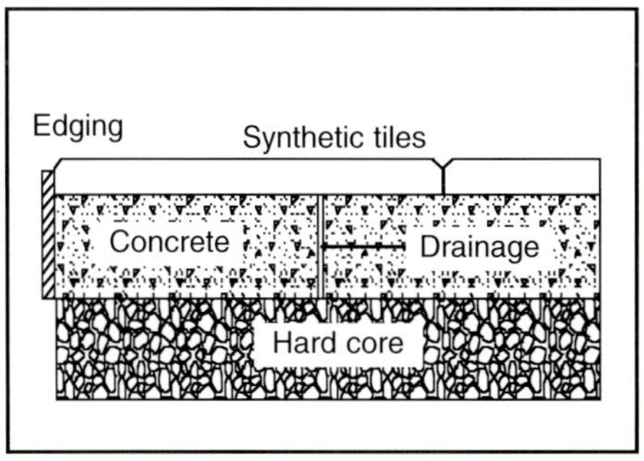

Fig.4.4 Synthetic surfacing

The provision of an impact absorbing surface is an expensive operation and the following points represent additional information on laying of impact absorbing surfaces:

1. Safety surfacing must be laid strictly in accordance with manufacturers' instructions.
2. Surfacing should be laid to slight and even falls to ensure that water is shed from the surface.
3. Care should be taken to ensure that the finished surface is left in a clean and uniform condition
4. Joints should be properly bonded and where tiles are used care should be taken to ensure that adjacent tiles are flush across the joints and with the top of the edging material
5. Any gaps between surfacing and play equipment should be filled with an appropriate filler material to match the surrounding surface.
6. Surfacing to be to the critical fall heights specified in BS 5696 Part 3 and indicated in the specification.
7. The finished level of the surface should be 25mm below the surrounding grass areas to allow mowing to take place without damage to the surface.
8. A record should be carefully made and kept of the type of surfacing finally laid together with all certificates and appropriate correspondence, particularly that relating to its critical height or impact absorbency. Where on larger sites or where

combinations of surfacing thickness or types have been used their precise locations should also be recorded as they were eventually installed.

9. For synthetic surfaces it is recommended that the product's name and "critical height" be permanently marked at a location on the surface for each type of surfacing.
10. For large synthetic Impact Absorbing Surfacing contracts it is recommended that a post installation inspection and on site test be undertaken to confirm the surfaces satisfactory installation and "critical height".
11. The contractor should reinstate all surrounding turf or hard surfaced areas on completion of the work to the satisfaction of the Works Service Manager.

4.4 IMPACT ABSORBING SURFACING - ESTIMATED COST INFORMATION

The following budget costs are taken from the NPFA Cost Guide 1995 edition (see 3.3)

LOOSE FILL SURFACES consisting of particulate tree bark 300mm deep laid on a filtration membrane over a freely draining foundation and retained by treated timber edging.

The following include supply, delivery, installation, and impact absorbing surfacing where necessary. All estimated costs are exclusive of VAT.

- Particulate tree bark
    - Small areas (approximately 50m^2) £50/m^2
    - Larger areas (approximately 150m^2) £45/m^2

- SYNTHETIC/RUBBER SURFACES (tile/in-situ) with a critical fall height (CFH) (tested in accordance with BS 7188) and sited on an existing suitable macadam or concrete base or to include the provision of a new base for the surface to be laid on.

For small areas (approximately 50 m^2)	Existing BASE/m^2	New BASE/m^2
≥1m CFH	£40 - £48	£60 - £73
≥2m CFH	£65 - £70	£85 - £95
≥2.5m	£70 - £85	£95 - £110

For larger areas (approximately 150m^2):	Existing BASE/m^2	New BASE/m^2
≥1m CFH	£35 - £45	£58 - £70
≥2m CFH	£50 - £65	£75 - £90
≥2.5m	£55 - £80	£80 - £105

(2.5m is the maximum fall height permitted by BS 5696)

4.5 STANDARDS

Impact absorbing surfaces are governed by BS 5696 and by BS 7188. Therefore, when a surface is installed, the supplier should be required to provide written confirmation that the surface has been tested in accordance with BS 7188 for determination of critical height, resistance to abrasive wear, slip resistance, resistance to indentation and ease of ignition and complies with the recommendations of BS 5696, Part 3; that if installed and maintained to the manufacturer's instruction, the surface will retain its impact absorbency for the full guarantee or warranty period. For loose fill surfaces such as tree bark it is only practical to test for determination of critical height and ease of ignition.

- Maintenance instructions should also be supplied and the installer should be directed to confirm that the surface has been installed to the manufacturer's instructions and recommendations

- Suppliers should provide a guarantee or warranty period of at least five years.

4.6 REPLACEMENT PRIORITIES

It is unlikely that sufficient funds will normally become available to allow Property Managers to undertake complete re-surfacing work on a significant number of play areas at one time. It is therefore presumed that most will wish to adopt a priority system for surface replacement in line with that for changing items of play equipment. It makes little sense to install a modern synthetic surface under a piece of equipment which has a life expectancy of less than five years; both should be replaced together within the five year period.

As a general principle in legal proceedings, there is an expectation that playground operators should have a reasonable programme of upgrading and replacement. While it may not be necessary for all upgrading work to be carried out at once, Property Managers should be able to produce a work schedule utilising as appropriate a rolling programme of replacement and improvements.

Nevertheless, as a general rule, priority for installing impact absorbing surfaces should be given to selected toddler playgrounds which have, or are expected to have, a high usage by very young children. Thereafter, priority should be given to surfaces under those pieces of equipment which are most associated with accidents. In order of importance these are:

1 Tower style slides over 2.5m high
2 Tower style slides under 2.5m high
3 Climbing structures and agility equipment over 1m in height
4 Swings
5 Cable runways
6 Climbing agility structures equipment under 1m in height
7 See-saws
8 Rocking and spring items
9 Roundabouts

5 A step-by-step approach to play area design, installation and maintenance for property managers

INTRODUCTION

The purpose of this chapter is to provide Property Managers and their staff with a comprehensive, step-by-step check list for the installation of new play areas, or the refurbishment of existing facilities, on their MQ estates. It should be used in conjunction with the specialist advice obtainable from EWCs and WSMs and should reflect, as far as is practicable, the wishes of the local community, and take account of any other facilities in the area provided by the local authority or other bodies.

Where specialist advice is obtained by either the EWC or WSM, the Property Manager must ensure that this does not lead to a conflict of interest. For example there must be a separation between independent advice and the procurement of works, to ensure financial probity and public accountability.

The complete process can be divided into eight separate stages although it may not always be either practical or necessary to take account of every step each time a play area project is contemplated.

Property Managers and their staff are advised that the Standard to be used for all aspects of playground management is BS5696 Play equipment intended for permanent installation outdoors, unless the item is not covered by the Standard. In this event the German Standard DIN7926 plus the technical recommendations of the National Playing Fields Association should be used.

BS5696 consists of the following three parts:-

- Part 1 - Methods of test
- Part 2 - Specification for construction and performance
- Part 3 - Code of practice for installation and maintenance

STAGE 1 - REVIEW OF EXISTING FACILITIES AND SAFETY AUDIT

The EWC is responsible for carrying out inspections of play areas to establish the condition and maintenance requirements. This will include the foreseeable replacement of any item or element, or if required the complete refurbishment of an area within the next ten years for inclusion in the Forward Maintenance Register.

The Property Manager may identify a need for a new play area to be provided; it would then be necessary to determine the outline requirements for the play facilities and, the order of cost and timing within the Forward Maintenance Register. This should be carried out by the EWC.

However, as explained in Chapter 1, the formal play area is but one part of the play environment so that the layout of parks and cycleways, the configuration of streets, planting, and the adaptation of natural features will all similarly contribute to children's development. They should, therefore, be reviewed at the same time as a play area project is being planned, particularly where a new MQ estate or major refurbishment scheme is contemplated. In the latter case, a new play area should always be included as an integral part of the project and the opportunity taken to maximise the play potential of the complete MQ environment.

The chance to design a new play area within a projected new estate will, however, be rare. Much more common will be the need to refurbish existing facilities. Here it will be necessary to undertake a safety audit of existing pieces of equipment and their surrounding surfaces to establish:

- The equipment's compliance with Standards and its life expectancy so that the requirement for, and degree of urgency of its replacement, can be assessed.

- The height, MUZ plus extent and quality of IAS of all equipment with more than a 5 year future, so that the need to change the surface before the equipment can be determined.

- The play value of the site (assess against Annex C).

The EWC should provide the necessary specialist advice and may obtain further assistance from specialist consultants, equipment manufacturers, Local Authorities, or the organisations listed in Annex A.

STAGE 2 - LOCAL CONSULTATION

Having established the probable scope and priority of a play area project, Property Managers are strongly advised to consult both the residents and children of the estate. The lessons learnt from past projects in the area and consultation with adjacent communities should be substituted for direct consultation.

The aim of Stage 2 is to determine the type of equipment which is likely to be most popular with the potential user and its possible layout, as well as changes or improvements to the surrounding area.

Fig. 5.1 Local consultation

Past experience has shown that children take a keen interest in the design of their play area and can contribute a great deal to this process although the transient nature of the military community may reduce interest levels in this respect.

Adults should also have a chance to state their preferences and their concerns (noise, vandalism, lack of supervision, etc) and at the same time, they can be invited to take an active part in the running of the playground (and any play store that may be planned) and its future maintenance.

For obvious reasons care should be taken to ensure that community expectations about the scope of a play area project and its time frame and funding are met as far as possible once they have been raised as a result of the consultative process.

STAGE 3 - PREPARATION OF A DESIGN BRIEF

When instructed by the Property Manager that the funds are available for the works to proceed, the EWC should prepare a design brief or Statement of Requisition. This should include a review of the existing play area site, and take into account the comments of local children and residents at the consultation stage. The outline requirements for the numbers/types of equipment/surfaces and anticipated life spans must be included.

The Property Manager will then issue the WSM with an order to proceed with the works, which includes both a financial limit and timescales for completion.

Responsibility for ensuring that the proper planning procedures have been followed by the WSM for play areas rests with the Property Manager (or in certain cases the Project Manager). In all cases they should seek the advice of the local DLA (Defence Land Agent) after the Design Brief has been prepared. The DLA will advise whether a NOPD (Notice of Proposed Development) is required and will consider at that stage whether Head Defence Lands Services (DLS) should be consulted.

The WSM (or Project Manager) is also responsible for preparing and, unless the DLA advises otherwise, submitting the NOPD to the Local Planning Authority. The Design Brief should indicate that the planning position has been established. The design brief should be issued to the WSM for further action once it is complete, although the Property Manager will remain responsible for priorities, finance and agreeing design changes.

STAGE 4 - PREPARATION OF TENDER DOCUMENTATION

In Stage 4 the WSM is responsible for translating the design brief into tender documentation. The Defence Works Services advise that this type of works service may be suitable for a "design and build" contract, and advise that such a strategy should be adopted.

STAGE 5 - OBTAINING AND EVALUATION OF TENDERS AND AWARDING CONTRACT

The WSM should next produce a short list of no more than 3 or 4 suitable firms. Having done so the WSM should seek and evaluate tenders with the Property Manager and then, on the latter's authority, let the contract.

In choosing equipment evaluate each item in terms of:

- play value (see Annex C)
- maintenance requirements
- replaceable components
- life expectancy
- durability
- cost

Suppliers should also be required to provide specific additional information on the equipment's compliance with British Standards and its warranty period (Chapter 3), and draw attention to any maintenance anomalies (Chapter 5 Stage 8).
Similarly, when installing new surfacing, the supplier should again confirm compliance with the British Standard in accordance with Chapter 4. Surfacing specifications should, in particular, indicate:

- Setting out areas
- Excavation work
- Edging materials
- Foundation material
- Sub-base material
- Method by which the surface will be laid.

For major new schemes and layouts to be prepared by external contract or design or undergoing a competitive tender submission from playground equipment manufacturers and suppliers, a submission paper should also be required. This should detail the play value of the scheme and its advantages to children and their play activities. On larger schemes a layout plan should also be required.

STAGE 6 - INSTALLATION OF EQUIPMENT AND SURFACING

Site supervision and security during installation work and surfacing should be managed in accordance with normal WSM procedures.

For obvious reasons it is important to ensure that children are unable to use recently installed equipment until it has been handed over by the WSM and the complete facility has been opened following the formal post-installation inspection. Until that point the site remains the contractor's legal responsibility.

STAGE 7 - ACCEPTANCE OF COMPLETED CONTRACT

Acceptance of a completed facility by the Property Manager following EWC inspection, once the WSM has ensured that the work has been carried out in accordance with BS 5696, should follow established procedures laid down in DWS Technical Bulletin, Handover of Completed Projects 53/94. Written confirmation that the equipment has been installed to the manufacturer's instructions and BS 5696 Part 3 should be obtained.

STAGE 8 - INSPECTION, MAINTENANCE AND ACCIDENT PROCEDURES

The need for regular inspections of play areas and their equipment, followed by effective maintenance and repair when it is needed, is self evident. However, this has been increasingly reinforced in recent years as courts have demanded proof of regular inspection, when litigation for play injuries is being heard. Proof can consist of written logs recording: playground inspections, repairs, amendments, new equipment installation dates and accident records. Such documentation should be kept for at least 10 years.

Inspections should take place at daily, quarterly and annual intervals. In addition MQ residents should be encouraged to report obvious faults to the Property Manager as early as possible. A sign with the appropriate contact number should always be prominently displayed in every playground to assist in this process, see section 5.5.3.

DAILY OR ROUTINE VISUAL INSPECTIONS

These should be undertaken by a member of the Property Manager's staff and recorded. The inspector undertaking this task should understand inspection principles and the correct positioning and use of the equipment items for the site.

Overall points should include the following:

- Each item's structure and its operational completeness
- Surface finish
- Consumable components
- Awareness of the dangers of sharp edges, entrapment and crush points
- Which parts should move and which should not
- Drainage points on the ground and for the equipment

The inspection should be undertaken to ensure that from day to day the site and its equipment remain fit for its intended purpose. It is not a dismantling inspection.

This routine daily inspection is to identify faults and hazards that may have occurred through wear and tear, weather conditions or through vandalism. Elements should be checked by following a standard routine using the acronym DEWS. This list is not exhaustive and needs to be regularly updated in light of site and operational experience.

Fig. 5.2 Damaged surface

D debris, litter, broken glass, dog or cat defecation, obstacles eg old shopping trolleys and that the playground and the equipment is clean eg no graffiti.

E elements, all present eg barriers, swing chains, seating slates, litter bins and their liners, slide steps.

W works, for example, the roundabout moves correctly, the swing seats and chains operate correctly and are not wrapped around the top bar

S surfacing, particularly impact absorbing surfacing is all clean and present.On loose fill impact absorbing surfaces, care should be taken to ensure that no debris is present within the surface, that wear ruts related to moving items such as swings have their surfacing redistributed to the correct levels.

Particular attention should be taken where new items of equipment are installed both from the "running in" period and the "honey potting" that will occur with children using the new item. Additional points to consider are tightening up of components, security of foundations and whether access and flow routes, barriers and seating positions work, or are creating potential problems.

Should any defects or problems be found the appropriate action should be taken eg. to prevent the use of unsafe equipment or to arrange for the removal of litter. All defects should be reported to the Property Manager to arrange for the necessary remedial work to be carried out.

QUARTERLY MAINTENANCE REPAIR AND SAFETY CHECKS

The WSM is required to undertake a maintenance, repair and safety check on a three monthly basis. This inspection is included in DWS Specification 005 (Property Management of the Defence Estate Issue 003)

The WSM should understand the checks and the correct positioning and use of the equipment items for the site. Overall points should include the following:

- Each item's structure and its operational completeness
- Surface finish
- Consumable components
- Awareness of the dangers of sharp edges, entrapment and crush points
- Which parts should move and which should not
- Drainage points on the ground and for the equipment

Fig. 5.3 Damaged swing chain

Fig. 5.4 Maintenance works

It should take into account servicing checks advised by the manufacturers of particular equipment elements and assess the overall operational condition of the items and the playground. This is a non dismantling inspection.

It is now becoming more common for items with moving parts to have "sealed for life" units. Replacement may be necessary after a specified period or be dependent upon intensity of use. Care should be taken to operate each and every item to its fullest extent to assess for signs of wear and the consequential need for a part to be replaced.

Elements should be checked by following a standard routine, and the full detail of this inspection should be recorded.

The operational inspection should be undertaken by following a standard routine using the acronym PRIMES. This list is not exhaustive and needs to be regularly updated in light of site and operational experience.

P perimeter of the overall playground boundary internally and externally and the perimeter to each item being inspected.

R rigid elements, stanchions, supports and structural members.

I individual elements for wear and completeness eg swing chain, swing seats. bolts, stair treads etc.

M moving items and elements eg rocking equipment, swings and their component parts including chains, shackle pins, bushes, etc.

E exterior finish of each item, eg paintwork, graffiti, splinters, etc.

S surfacing, hard, natural and impact absorbing surfacing.

Should any defects or problems be found they should if possible be corrected there and then eg by picking up litter. All actions should be recorded and those not able to be corrected there and then reported to the Property Manager immediately for action.

ANNUAL INSPECTIONS

These should be carried out by the EWC using an independent specialist to ascertain, at intervals not exceeding 12 months, the overall level of safety of the playground and the equipment on it. This inspection is included in DWS Specification 005 (Property Management of the Defence Estate Issue 003)

Evidence of rotting or corrosion should be carefully checked together with the structural stability of the item and its foundations together with the surfacing that is provided.

This inspection is a non dismantling inspection and will be expected to highlight specific areas that will require more detailed investigation or dismantlement or excavation to be implemented by the Property Manager.

Results of the annual inspection should be carefully recorded and the actions or recommendations acted upon. It is suggested that a "site diary" is developed to log all inspections and where applicable subsequent maintenance in one document. Details of independent specialists able to undertake this work can be obtained from Annex A.

Additional inspections as advised by the manufacturer may also be necessary for specific elements of the equipment although these may be able to be combined with another inspection or dismantling check in order to save resources.

Planned maintenance of equipment carried out by the WSM should include:

- lubrication of moving parts
- replacement of loose-fill materials
- any other servicing requirements included in the suppliers' literature or advised by the manufacturer

The EWC should comment on these aspects as part of the annual inspection.

All maintenance tasks should also be recorded against a unique equipment number. This maybe undertaken be using computer information technology. There are now a number of software programs specialising in this area and details can be obtained from Annex A. Such records, together with inspection reports and installation details will make up the site record which should be kept by the WSM.

Experience has shown that aspects most likely to constitute a major hazard are:

- Damage, to or failure of, safety panels, barriers and guard rails
- Exposure of equipment mechanisms
- The dispersal, loss, breakdown, or non provision of impact absorbing surfaces

Such faults should be repaired within 24 hours if possible and the repairs recorded. Where a fault could cause an accident eg a missing step to a slide, the Property Manager should be immediately notified and the item immediately put out of action so as to prevent children it. It must be recognised that a notice or fencing will not normally stop children using an item, indeed it will often encourage children to investigate it further. Consequently the only way normally is to remove the item.

Property Managers must be aware of their overall responsibilities under the Health & Safety at Work Act.

ACCIDENTS

Should a serious accident occur it is important that the Property Manager is immediately informed and that the details of the incident, plus the details of any injured parties and witnesses, are carefully recorded. It is further recommended that in the case of a serious accident Property Managers have a safety inspection undertaken. The record of this should be kept for at least ten years. From this information any faults should be rectified immediately.

This is an ongoing exercise and all property managers should collate their information and permanently record it in their record book. This information should be used to upgrade the safety of not only individual playgrounds but all playgrounds that the Property Manager is responsible for. Information regarding accidents that occur, should be forwarded to the Health & Safety Advisor at DWS HQ, who will assess the incident and inform other Property Managers with the issue of a Safety Notice if appropriate.

As will be seen from Annex D there are a number of important lessons that can be learnt to reduce the severity of accidents. By far the most important is the provision of facilities to reduce the severity of accidents resulting from falls. This may be done by the provision of appropriate impact absorbing surfaces, effective barriers and the removal of trip points.

It will also be seen that certain ranges of equipment notably climbing frames, slides and swings are related to the more numerous and often most serious accidents. This is not to recommend against their provision in a playground but to advise on their popularity and need to ensure their correct operational safety.

For items requiring impact absorbing surfacing to meet current standards of safety chapter 4 and section 4.6 will provide assistance in the selection of priority items.

Annex A Organisations specialising in playground provision, design, layout, management, inspection and maintenance.

The following organisations are able to offer EWCs and WSMs independent specialist advice in relation to provision of children's play area facilities:

A1 THE NATIONAL PLAYING FIELDS ASSOCIATION

The National Playing Fields Association is the national organisation which has specific responsibility for acquiring, protecting and improving playing fields, playgrounds and playspace where they are most needed, and for those who need them most - in particular, children of all ages and people with disabilities. The NPFA is an independent charity offering advice concerning safety, construction and design as well as producing an independent playground safety inspection service. The NPFA relies on donations from the public and the generosity of its supporters.

NPFA Playground Services Ltd (NPFA PSL) is a company wholly owned and set up by the National Playing Fields Association any profits made are returned to the Charity to promote and continue its aims and objectives. NPFA PSL provides a range of commercial and advisory services for playground managers. These include:

- Safety audits, safety checks
- Log book or site diary inspection service
- Annual inspections
- Post-installation inspections
- Playground monitoring software
- Training
- Accident inspections Legal and Expert Witness Advice
- General information and advice

National Playing Fields Association
25 Ovington Square, London SW3 1LQ.
Telephone: 0171 584 6445. Fax: 0171 581 2402

A2 ROYAL SOCIETY FOR THE PREVENTION OF ACCIDENTS

RoSPA is Europe's largest organisation which offers a range of services in:

- Water and Leisure Safety
- Occupational Safety
- Home Safety
- Product Safety
- Road Safety
- School Safety

For children's play areas the Society provides inspections, accident investigation, training and advice. RoSPA provides post-installation and safety checks for specialised soft play areas in public, restaurants and other leisure facilities including the larger adventure areas. A Certificate of good Practice is available for new facilities meeting the Society's standards.

Royal Society for the Prevention of Accidents
Cannon House
The Priory Queensway
Birmingham
B4 6BS

Telephone: 0121 200 2461. Fax.: 0121 200 1254

A3 ASSOCIATION OF PLAY INDUSTRIES

The Association of Play Industries is a trade organisation representing British manufacturers and distributors of playground equipment and surfaces. The Association is strongly committed to the promotion of quality and safety in playgrounds, and it is a condition of membership that companies should comply with all relevant British and European Standards, and should encourage end users such as schools and local authorities to insist upon them. The Association includes over 80% of the British play industry.

Association of Play Industries
Federation House
National Agricultural Centre
Stoneleigh Park
Warwickshire
CV8 2RF

Telephone: 01203 414999. Fax: 01203 414990

Annex B Reading list

The following are publications that have been referred to.

Health and Safety at Work Act, 1981
Environmental Protection Act, 1991

DWS Landscaping manual published by HMSO
DWS Parking and access manual published by HMSO

Ministry of Agriculture Fisheries & Food - Poisonous plants and Fungi
ISBN 011 2427189

British Standard 5696 Play equipment intended for permanent installation outdoors Part 1 Methods of test, Part 2 Specification for construction and performance, Part 3 Code of practice for installation and maintenance.

British Standard BS 7188 British Standard method of test for Impact Absorbing Playground Surfaces.

Deutsche Institut Fur Normung DIN 7926, playground equipment for children, Part 1 Concepts, Supplement 1, Terminology Part 2 Swings, Part 3 Slides, Part 4 Cable railways, Part 5 Carousels

NPFA, Dogs and Recreation Policy Guidelines, 1994

NPFA, The Six Acre Standard, 1993

NPFA, Taking The Lead, 1994

NPFA, Kickabout Areas, 1980.

NPFA, The NPFA Cost Guide 1995 for Sport, Buildings and Children's Play Facilities incorporating Listings of Main contractors and Suppliers as supplied to and used by The Building Cost Information Service of the RICS and the Sports Council (annually revised).

NPFA TECHNICAL ADVICE NOTICES (TANS)

TAN 1	Children's Play equipment - BS 5696 recommendations on extent of impact absorbing surface area (revised 120193)
TAN 2	Children's Play equipment - BS 5696 recommendations on fencing surrounding swings
TAN 3	Children's Play equipment - BS 5696 recommendations on handgrip dimensions
TAN 4	Children's Play equipment - BS 5696 recommendations on minimum use zones (revised 080193)
TAN 5	Children's Play equipment - BS 5696 recommendations on the sliding surfaces and retaining sides of slides
TAN 6	Children's play equipment - inspection failures
TAN 7	Fencing of children's playgrounds
TAN 9	NPFA Interpreted BS 5696 Dimension (revised 080193)
TAN 10	Overhead power lines, playing fields and play areas
TAN 11	Tree bark as impact absorbing surfacing for children's play areas
TAN 12	Playground inspections - playground equipment and surfacing

TAN 13	Playground equipment inspection methodology
TAN 14	Playgrounds - trim trails
TAN 15	Portable goal posts
TAN 16	Skateboard areas
TAN 18	Tree trunks as play equipment
TAN 19	Wicksteed Sputnik roundabout (update 140394)
TAN 20	Children's play Equipment - BS 5696 and NPFA recommendations on slip resistant surfaces for ladders, stairs and ramps
TAN 22	Notes on the construction and maintenance of children's sand pits
TAN 25	Children's play equipment - remedying slippery wood surfaced footways
TAN 27	Children's playground equipment not recommended by the NPFA

Annex C Play value assessment

INTRODUCTION

The play value of a playground, whether existing or proposed, may be assessed by using the following NPFA method. There is no fixed pass or fail score. The purpose is to produce a relative score that can be compared to other playgrounds.

Play value scores can assist in assessing the relative value of one tender against another. The purpose is to establish whether one tender offers a substantially greater or lower play value than another. Schemes of similar play value may then be further considered against personal preferences.

Three distinct areas are addressed to cover site and equipment features plus play co-operation. These have had incorporated into them a wide range of play, learning, social and developmental opportunities together with safety, supervision and environmental aspects. The list is by no means exhaustive and may be further developed and tuned to the needs of the operator.

Where an item does not meet the necessary standards of safety eg no impact absorbing surface the item should still be scored and the number of items not complying recorded with the final play value score.

INSTRUCTION FOR USE:

For each playground or tender submission firstly consider the playground's overall site features and award a score per bullet point for the overall playground. There is no requirement to award the maximum score if it is considered that it is not appropriate.

For example, when considering "Informal supervision" a site that is not so well overlooked would be awarded a lower score than a playground that was. A max. figure is given in order to promote a balanced playground. For example a playground should not have a high score because of its 15 park benches and 6 litter bins while the only physical play equipment is one seesaw and a slide. Each bullet point's description is fairly broad to allow it to be interpreted rather than provide an exhaustive list that would be very difficult to use for all schemes without appropriate training. Professional assessments can be obtained through organisations listed in Annex A.

Then proceed to score the playground's equipment item by item. Finally award an additional score, if appropriate, for play co-operation. The score for site features, equipment features and play co-operation are then totalled to produce the playground's play value score.

SITE FEATURES

Score one point per item or group of items.

The scores are for the overall playground, even if it contains within it toddler, junior or major sections unless specifically allowed as in the case of: distinct playground sections for toddlers etc., seating, footpaths, lighting fencing and pedestrian gates.

- Informal adult supervision (max. 4)
  e.g. the site is well overlooked from the front doors of housing
- Ground contouring, sculpturing, etc. (max. 2)
- Planting (max. 1)

- Environmental planting (max. 1 if present)
- Vehicle safety (max. 1)
- Noise pollution (max. 1 if none, 0 if present)
- Traffic pollution (max. 1 if none, 0 if present)
- Sunny/shady (max.1 for mixed, 0 for sunny or shady)
- Child seat (or a group of child seats) (1 per overall playground or 1 per distinct toddler/junior/major playground section)
- Adult seat (or a group of adult seats) (As above)
- Internal hard surfaced footpaths linking equipment or items (As above)
- Lighting (As above)
- Fencing (to restrict dogs entering) (As above)
- Pedestrian self closing gate (As above)
- Vehicular gate (for maintenance) (max. 1)
- Sign advising on the site management and excluding dogs (max. 1)
- Bicycle resting points, where they may be locked (max. 1)
- Litter bins (max. 1)
- Shelter for adults and children i.e. a roof structure for rain or sun protection, this should not form part of a play equipment item (max. 1)
- Layout of the site and the way it works (max. 2)
- Visual appeal (max. 2)
- Site condition(graffiti, vandalism, litter etc) (max. 1)
- Play challenge items (max 2)

EQUIPMENT FEATURES

Score 1 point per item.

The max scores are per playground or, if the sections are sufficiently distinct, per toddler, junior or major sections for the playground. Items that directly link, e.g. a series of balance beams, or a series of items that in effect form one activity e.g. stepping logs should be treated as one item. Multi-use or combination equipment e.g. a play structure containing a slide, fireman's pole, clatter bridge etc. should be split up and treated as individual items. Features providing an access route such as a ladder or stairs are not counted.

- Rocking, per user position (max. 3)
- Gliding e.g. an aerial runway (max. 3)
- Rotating, single or twin user item (max. 2)
- Rotating, multi-user user item, per user position (max. 2)
- Sliding, conventional slide (max. 3)
- Sliding, hand grip e.g. a fireman's pole (max. 2)
- Swinging (max. 2)
- Swinging, single point suspension swing (max. 3)
- Balancing (max. 1)
- Jumping (max. 1)
- Climbing e.g. agility items such as climbing bars or overhead bars and nets (max. 2)
- Agility bridges e.g. clatter or suspension style (max. 1)
- Crawling e.g. short tunnels (max. 1)
- Viewing platforms e.g. platforms on towers or bubble domes (max. 1)
- Ball play area (max. 2)
- Wheel play area eg for bicycles and skateboards (max. 2)

Score 1 point per item or group of items. The max. scores are for the overall playground.

- Sandpit or sandbox (max. 3)
- Sand play table or item to assist in sand play (max. 3)
- Water play e.g. a water table or pump item (max. 3)
- Social play e.g. a play hut or group of child seats and a table (max. 2)
- Educational or learning feature e.g. abacus (max. 2)
- Items for children with special needs (max. 2)
- Ground graphics e.g. hopscotch (max. 2)
- Items generating or reflecting sound (max. 2)

Annex D Accident statistics compiled from documented reports by the NPFA

The following pie charts provide information on the types of accidents and injuries that have been documented by the NPFA. When studying accident types the most numerous are those accidents that occur as a result of a fall. The following list provides summary information that will assist in deciding the priority order of addressing improvements to children's playground equipment that does not meet current Standards. It should be read in conjunction with section 4.6 relating to replacement priorities and impact absorbing surfacing.

The types and percentage of accidents reported to the NPFA are shown below:-

- Falls 69%
- Entrapment 15%
- Struck by item 3%
- Other 13%

Other accidents:-

Of the other accidents reported to the NPFA, a significant proportion are entrapments, the majority of which have been under roundabouts.

Of the accidents documented by the NPFA a significant number are associated with falls onto hard surfaces. The following items of equipment have been identified as those most obviously linked with such accidents:-

- Slides 36%
- Climbing Frames 24%
- Swings 19%
- Overhead Horizontal Ladders 4%
- Other 17%

Injuries:-

A chart is provided showing the types of injuries sustained. It should be stressed that due to their nature it tends to be the more serious injuries that are reported and documented, the vast number of minor accidents are not reported and hence not included in these figures. The NPFA is currently investigating this area of work, in an effort to better understand accident cause and the nature of injuries, to further improve playground safety.

Fig. D1 Accident statistics compiled from documented report by the NPFA¬

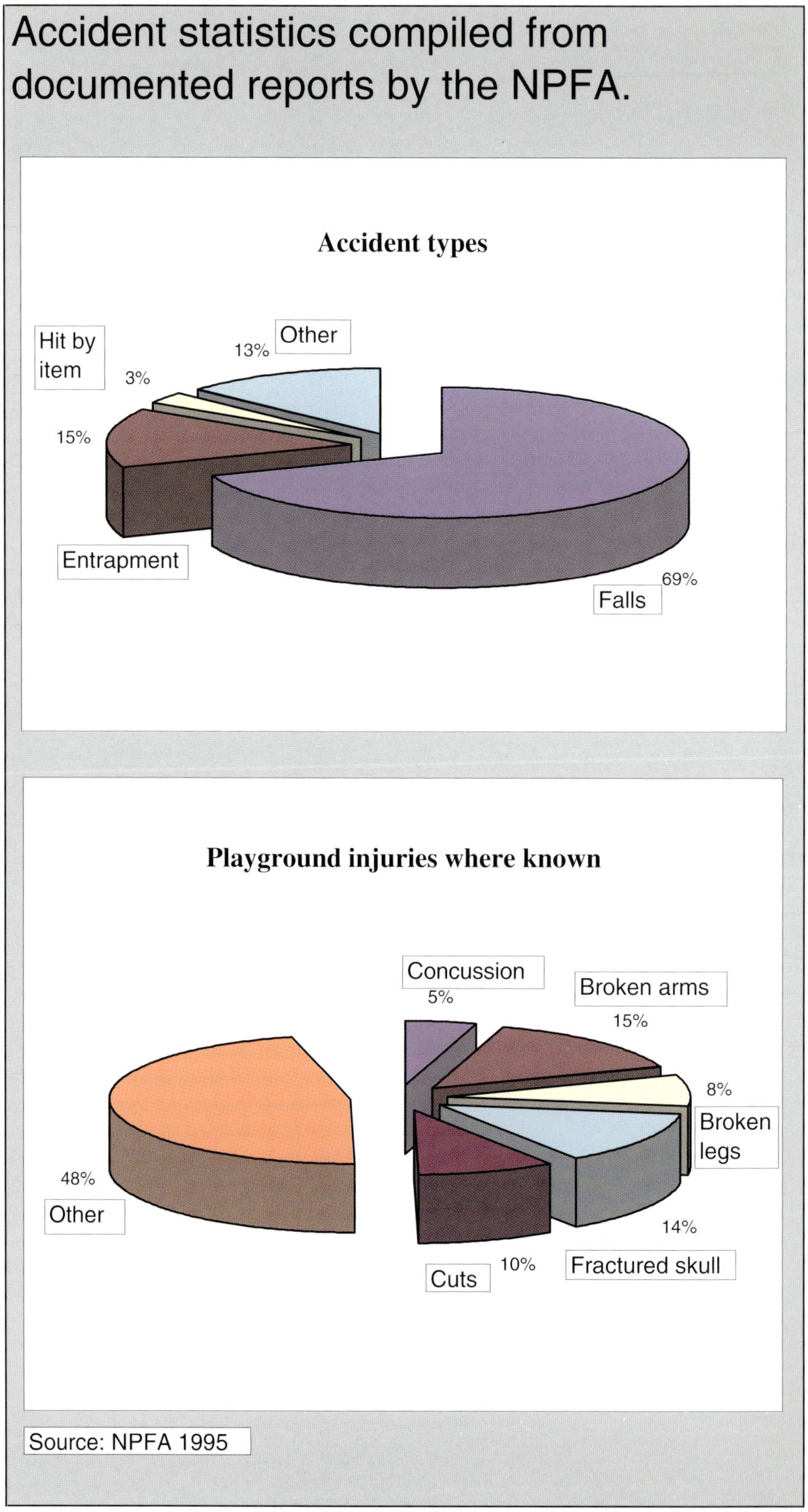

Fig. D2 Accidents in relation to equipment types

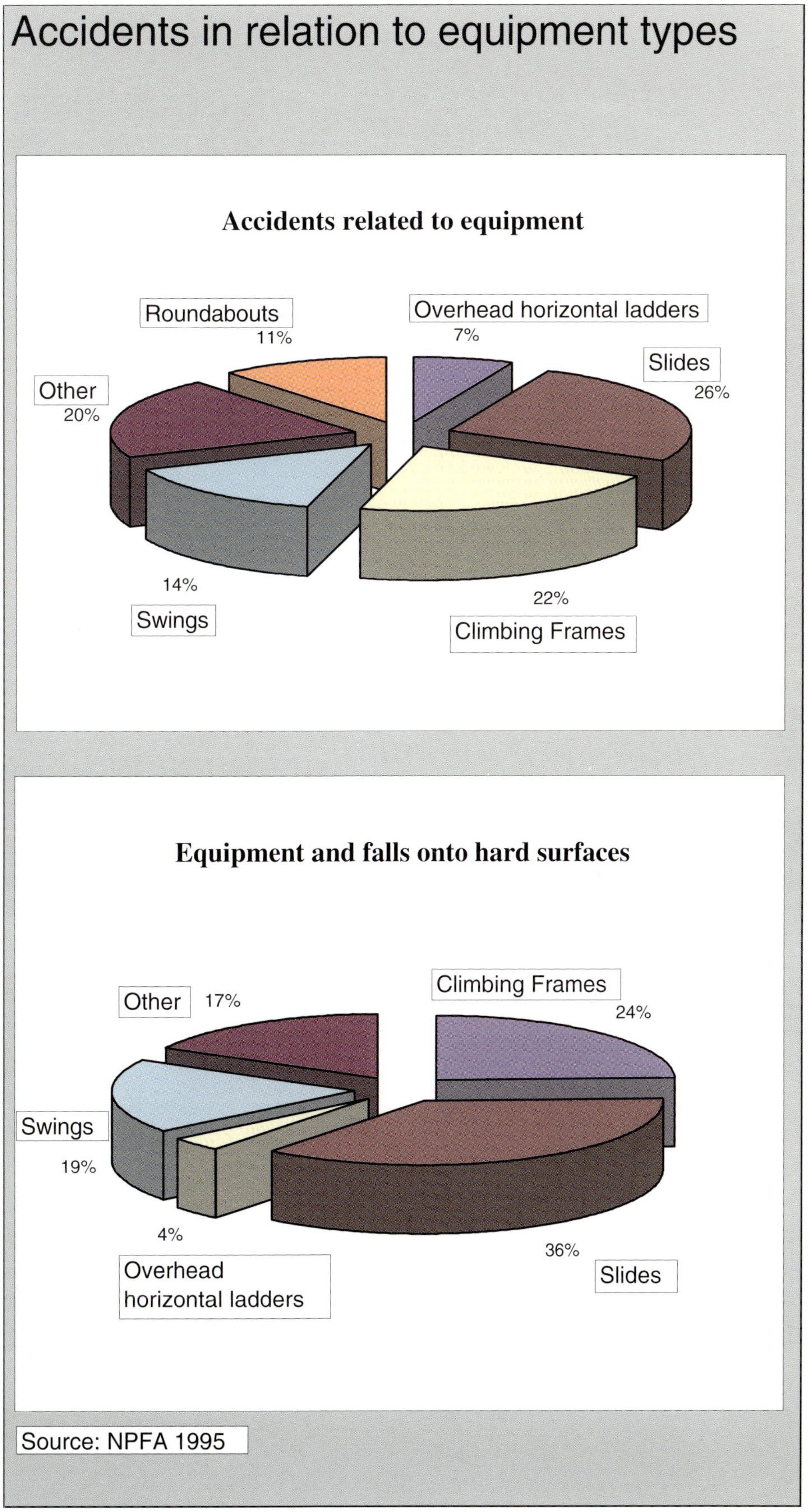

Annex E Additional information for kickabout areas, wheeled play opportunities and places for teenagers to meet

The main challenge, in design and layout terms, is to achieve a sensible balance between the often conflicting interests of play value, safety, aesthetics and disturbances to nearby residents.

There is no single design solution. With imagination and awareness of the underlying principles the opportunities are endless.

The notes set out below are intended to serve to illustrate the major underlying principles, and provide illustrative design criteria and suggestions. The properties and nature of individual locations will play an important part in deciding a specific design solution.

E1 NOTES FOR A KICKABOUT AREA

E1.1 Description

The term 'Kickabout' is widely used to describe a whole variety of different facilities. In this context the term is used to describe a facility for children's active play with a ball. It is not intended for formal or informal sports e.g. five-a-side soccer. It is intended to provide a safe and purpose built facility as a substitute to the form of ball play activities children play in the road and at other inappropriate places.

E1.2 Typical uses & observations

Children enjoy both simulating some of the more spectacular aspects of recognised sports and playing improvised ball games. The two most common balls used are a plastic football and tennis ball. These are readily available and easily adaptable. e.g. a football becomes a netball becomes a basketball - a tennis ball becomes a hockey ball becomes a cricket ball.

Fig. E.1 Improvised ball games

The number of children normally involved at any one time ranges from 1 to 7 with 3 to 5 being most common. It is comparatively rare for groups of more than 7 children to play ball games together, and comparatively rare for them to organise themselves into two opposing sides.

More often than not children's ball games involve 'facilitators', 'attackers' and a 'defence' with the players taking it in turns to fulfil the various roles. Perhaps the most common example is based on football. Where 2 wingers (facilitators) float the ball across the goal mouth. Where 2 strikers (attackers) attempt to score goals with fancy overhead kicks, diving headers and volleys on the run. Whilst 1 goalkeeper (the defence) attempts spectacular diving saves and more often than not spends a great deal of time retrieving the ball from afar before passing the ball back to the wingers to start the cycle again.

It is also very common for children to play ball on their own. This nearly always involves the use of an improvised 'knock up' or 'rebound wall' as a substitute for a 'playing partner'. Most of the ball games children play are relatively low key and involve very little space and a minimum buffer zone to protect against disturbances to nearby residents and safety to users of adjacent play opportunities.

The exception to this is also the most common and popular ball game children play. i.e. based on football and described above. Whilst this ball game requires a relatively small active space it normally requires a large buffer zone and/or some form of 'ball retention' measure.

Learning from this we can conclude that children do not at every location need specialised facilities, but they must be reasonably close to home and sufficiently attractive and functional to better the alternatives at inappropriate places they will otherwise use.

E1.3 DESIGN, LAYOUT & CONTENT

The four main features of a Kickabout are: the play structure, the active zone, the buffer zone and ball retaining measures. The play structure and its surfacing occupies an area of approx. 20 sq. metres (5m dia circle). the essential ingredients are a goal mouth, basket/net ball hoop and 'knock up' wall. Easily added extras are hopscotch markings and cricket stumps and endless others. One essential design element from a play value perspective is to ensure there can be few disputes as to whether, for example, a goal has been scored or not. Hence painted lines on a flat surface are poor play value compared to goal mouth or cricket wicket several inches in front of the flat surface. Portable goal posts should not be used as serious injuries and a number of deaths have resulted from such items toppling over.

- Goal Mouth - 2m high x 3.5m wide preferably with a firm surface such as macadam
- Knock up wall - a solid flat structure - 1.2m high x 3m wide
- Basket/net ball post, backboard and hoop

E1.3.1 The active zone

A minimum rectangular area of approx. 30m x 20m is required - 45m x 30m is better. The play structure being located midway along the longest edge and inset approx. 5m. Where space is limited the active area can be shared by (say) formal sports pitch provided the play structure should be at least 2.5m clear of the pitch. This layout simply restricts use of the pitch during the few hours per week it is formally in use. Groundsmen quite like this when they realise the facility is discouraging children from using the formal pitch goal mouth they are desperately trying to maintain between matches.

E1.3.2 Buffer zone

There are two specific instances where a buffer zone is required. The first is to protect nearby residents and is catered for within the overall standards for a NEAP. The second is to protect other users of adjacent play facilities.

Buffer zone

A distance of approx. 25m is normally sufficient to ensure any football, for example, has lost most of its velocity and can do no more harm than startle anyone it may hit. If adequate ball retention measures have been taken then no additional buffer zone may be required. In choosing the location and orientation of the active area and ball play structure, due regard should be given to problems arising from sloping land, strong prevailing winds, directing play away from houses, roads and other potential hazards.

Ball retaining measures

In most circumstances fencing a minimum of 3m high & 7.5m wide would be suitable. If located close to or as part of the play structure - preferably higher, say 4 to 5 metres if required to protect properties, roads etc. From a distance of 40 plus metres galvanised or preferably black plastic coated heavy gauge chain link fencing (ball retention measure) is hardly noticeable and not a particular eyesore. Always provide a means through, rather than around the fencing, for children to fetch the ball the fence failed to retain. They will make their own if you do not provide one. Clear vandal-resistant plastic sheeting with green stripes (as often used for bus shelters) suitably supported is less visually obtrusive and can be coated in solutions that makes the removal of graffiti a great deal easier than wooden or metal flat surfaces; this is useful for knock up walls and basketball back boards. Besides its aesthetic value the use of see through structures is important for safety and security of the NEAP.

Further details on the construction can be found in the NPFA Publication "Kickabout Areas".

E1.3.4 NPFA multigames wall

For sites requiring a facility more orientated towards sport and a wide range of ball game activities for casual, training or even professional use the NPFA have developed a specialist Multigames Wall. The NPFA Multigames Wall has a number of innovative features to attract a variety of users. These include:

- goal posts and tennis nets shown in coloured brick to actual sizes
- timber cricket stumps and coloured plastic target panels built into the wall to help aiming skills - there's no argument if you hit the panel or stumps because of the different sound
- sections of angled brick to deflect balls at odd angles, bringing an element of surprise into play
- basketball or netball rings and backboards (correct size and height) to cater for the growing popularity of those sports
- the use of synthetic grass surfacing to overcome the problem of ground erosion - common on cricket wickets and in football goal mouths

Fig. E.2 Multigames Wall

The first Multigames Wall was built at the Tidworth Garrison, forming part of the provision for the married quarters estate where a large number of large families are quartered.

Since then its popularity has spread and to date 13 other NPFA Multigames Walls have been built throughout England and Wales. Full details together with a coloured brochure further describing this facility are available from the NPFA.

E2 NOTES FOR WHEELED PLAY:

E2.1 Description

Wheeled play in this context refers to an active play facility for children to use with cycles, skateboards and roller skates etc.

Fig. E.3 BMX Cycling

It is not intended as a substitute for BMX tracks or stunt areas, skateboard parks or roller skating rinks.

It is intended to provide a safe and attractive substitute for the type of wheeled play activity for children dependent on the fashion or trend of the day. These are traditionally played in the street, at underpasses and anywhere else they can find a land formation suitable to practise the basic skills.

Typical Uses and Observations: Children throughout the ages have always enjoyed wheeled play activities. Fortunately, the basic wheeled play structure required lends itself equally to use by cycles, skateboards and roller skates etc. and is thus not limited by particular crazes, trends or fashions of the day and survives the test of time.

Contrary to popular opinion, very low key and very safe structures and facilities are all that is required to achieve a very high play value for a very wide age range and associated range of abilities. This is best evidenced by observation of the improvised facilities at inappropriate and potentially unsafe places that children use when no purpose built facility exists close to their home.

Children are not by nature masochistic and go out of their way to avoid pain. Overall they have a great respect for known danger and have a native sense of restricting their activities to, at the most, that which marginally exceeds the limits of their own known ability. An excellent example of this is apparent when adults attempt to provide training and supervision for a young child's transition from riding a tricycle to a bicycle. Far from holding them back it is necessary to reassure them they are safe. The vast majority of accidents to children are caused by factors outside their full awareness or control. At an early age children become very aware of the dangers of cycles etc. in their own use / control and limit their activity accordingly.

Sadly, awareness of other traffic etc. and the possible safety implications take much longer to appreciate and fully understand. Besides a child's preoccupation with the activity at hand always runs a risk of that momentary loss of attention to all that is going on or around and about.

Children's play on wheels involves travelling at speed, raising one or both wheels off the ground, manoeuvring around obstacles and over a variety of slopes and gradients. Essentially it is not a race and the competitive element is expressed through showing off and development of skills. Counter to popular fear, younger children do not attempt to compete with older children, rather they mimic their activity in a modified form within the limits of their own known ability. e.g. an older child may well safely lift the front wheels of a cycle into the air and peddle on for some distance as if on a monocycle. a younger child will simply attempt to lift the front wheel and drop it immediately back to the ground achieving a lift of only an inch or two at best. The expression of self satisfaction and achievement remains the same for both younger and older child.

E2.2 DESIGN, LAYOUT & CONTENT

A 1.8m wide track with a length of approximately 100m (smaller circuits are often perfectly adequate and in no way affect the potential usage) constructed with a firm bound surface such as consolidated hoggin or where funds are available, macadam . Macadam, or preferably hot rolled asphalt, is essential for activities with small wheels such as skateboards. A track shape with continuous loop or better still a figure of eight is most popular.

If a figure of eight circuit is used then the cross over point should be an over and under arrangement. This is easily achieved by use of a standard bridge structure available from several major play equipment manufacturers along with a degree of land formation to ensure adequate height clearance for users on the underpass through route. Ideally the track should be raised on a mound varying in height from 0.5m to a maximum of 1.0m above normal ground level with appropriate cambers wherever corners are present. On route single and double mounds between 200mm and 400mm high above the track level are desirable provided they are placed on relatively straight sections of the track. When double mounds are used, the distance between the mounds should be such that a very young child's bike can ride smoothly over them without the necessity for a wheel to leave the ground. e.g. centres of the mounds approx. 0.75 metres apart if 200mm high and 1.25m apart if 400mm high. In turn this presents an exciting and safe obstacle for older children to 'jump'. A raised mound (stopping off, observation point) is desirable. This is best placed at a high point, where the entire track can be seen, and just offset such that users on the main track can by-pass those using the mound. The mound need only be 0.5m higher than the track and approx. 3m in diameter. There are many other features relating to specialisms for specific wheeled activities and these can and should usefully be explored with the children themselves who are often far more aware of current trends than adults.

Observation clearly demonstrates that even when children of different ages and abilities use the facility at the same time they are extraordinarily careful to only circulate in one direction and are very sensitive to each other. Whenever an individual or small group of individuals are insensitive to other users; then the other users nearly always move on to another activity and await a time when they can use the facility safely.

There is no requirement for a buffer zone above the normal requirement for a NEAP. What is required is a safe access with chicanes if necessary to reduce speed through or adjacent to other play features at the NEAP.

E3 NOTES FOR A MEETING PLACE

E3.1 Description

In this context a meeting place is a passive and sheltered play facility where teenagers can meet, sit and chat. It also serves as an area for adults accompanying children to use. It is not a building with fixtures and fittings. It is a sheltered bench with just minimal protection against the rain and wind. It is a purpose built substitute for the street corner, entrance hall or service area of a block of flats etc. where teenagers will meet in all weathers outdoors and close to home.

Fig. E.4 Meeting places

E3.2 Design, layout & contents

A simple bench with minimal but effective protection from the rain and wind is all that is required.

Modern bus shelters with only very minor alterations provide an excellent example of the design criteria. Also robust open sided timber or metal shelters are available from playground manufacturers.

A three sided structure constructed of vandal resistant clear plastic sides, a lean-to roof, and supported on legs under which users and passers by are aware of each others presence, containing a standard park bench made of inflammable material. The shelter should be served by at least secondary lighting and have informal surveillance from adjacent houses. No special buffer zone requirements are necessary above those normally pertaining to a NEAP. Its orientation should be to give protection from the most common prevailing winds experienced in the area, with views over other adjacent play features and facing housing providing informal surveillance. There should be clear sight lines for at least 20m on footpaths leading to and from the shelter. The shelter need only be 3m long by 1 to 1.5m deep and 2m high.

Chemical solutions for painting on indestructible clear plastic are available to considerably ease the removal of any graffiti.

First Edition published 1992
Second Edition 1995
ISBN 0 11 772459 9

This document is catalogued in the DWS Publications Index under the following key words:

Playgrounds

Index

(Main sections are shown with page numbers in bold)

T

V

W

Printed in the United Kingdom for HMSO
Dd. 298554 C35 10/95